JON C. STOTT

Wild BLUEBERRY *Summer*

More Upper Michigan Moments and Memories

Photography by Deb Le Blanc

Modern History Press

Ann Arbor, MI

Wild Blueberry Summer: More Upper Michigan Moments and Memories
Copyright © 2025 by Jon C. Stott. All Rights Reserved.
Photography by Deb Le Blanc

ISBN 979-8-89656-027-2 paperback
ISBN 979-8-89656-028-9 hardcover
ISBN 979-8-89656-029-6 eBook

Published by
Modern History Press
5145 Pontiac Trail
Ann Arbor, MI 48105

www.ModernHistoryPress.com
info@ModernHistoryPress.com
Tollfree 888-761-6268

Distributed by Ingram (USA/CAN/AU), Bertram's Books (UK/EU)
Audiobook available Audible.com and iTunes

Library of Congress Cataloging-in-Publication Data

Names: Stott, Jon C. author
Title: Wild blueberry summer : more Upper Michigan moments and memories / Jon C. Stott.
Description: Ann Arbor, MI : Modern History Press, 2025. | Includes index.
    | Summary: "This travelogue picks up where "Summers at the Lake" left off as the author recounts summers with family at Crooked Lake in Michigan's Upper Peninsula. He also recalls boyhood memories at Shawnigan Lake on Vancouver Island, Canada,"-- Provided by publisher.
Identifiers: LCCN 2025011040 (print) | LCCN 2025011041 (ebook) | ISBN 9798896560272 paperback | ISBN 9798896560289 hardcover | ISBN 9798896560296 eBook
Subjects: LCSH: Stott, Jon C.--Travel--Michigan--Upper Peninsula | Upper Peninsula (Mich.)--Description and travel | LCGFT: Autobiographies
Classification: LCC F572.N8 S76 2025 (print) | LCC F572.N8 (ebook) | DDC
    977.4/904092 $a B--dc23/eng/20250422
LC record available at https://lccn.loc.gov/2025011040
LC ebook record available at https://lccn.loc.gov/2025011041

Contents

Table of Figures

To my Crooked Lake friends and neighbors and to my Yooper friends—thank you for making my summers so enjoyable

—Jon C. Stott

In memory of Sunny, a wonderful companion on many years of photo shoots

—Deb Le Blanc

Foreword by Sharon M. Kennedy

Continuing what can only be called his tradition of writing poetic prose, Jon Stott invites readers to join him on another journey to his Little Cabin in the Big Woods in *Wild Blueberry Summer*, a sequel to his *Summers at the Lake*. Drawing on memories that brought this Canadian professor to Michigan's Upper Peninsula, Stott recalls summers when his parents crossed the border to the United States in search of an American Utopia. Although they loved their time spent at Shawnigan Lake on Vancouver Island off British Columbia, they were eager to discover what Michigan had to offer.

Years later, when Stott was married and the father of two children, the return of summer signaled freedom from his classrooms. He and his wife scouted new adventures and found Crooked Lake near Munising. By chance they came upon the cabin that would become theirs. It was a magical place deep in the woods where visitors had to travel through rough terrain to reach, but it was worth the bumps and ruts along the way. The day began with the call of loons awakening them and hastening their refreshing morning swim in the pristine lake. After breakfast, they hiked through the woods where trees, ferns, wild-flowers and berries greeted them. Evenings brought campfires and visits with neighbors who became friends and returned each year.

In *Wild Blueberry Summer*, Stott begins with a quote from *The Dispatches from Naples Ancient Shore* by Shirley Hazzard: "One achieves a slow, indelible intimacy with a place, learning to match its moods with one's own." This is an accurate summation of how he feels about Crooked Lake and his attachment to the modest cabin and its surroundings. To understand what touches his heart is to understand the man and his appreciation of the things life offers to all who are willing to accept them. It was not a mansion that caught his attention, but a simple building that held promises.

Picking wild blueberries on a sunny summer day is one of the pleasures he and his family enjoyed. Stott's a widower now and his children are grown. Sometimes his daughter, Clare, accompanies him and they share memories of days gone by. The tiny berries, so abundant and sweet, are picked with care and savored in muffins or sprinkled on breakfast cereals. Some are frozen and taken back to their home Stott has named the City of Pavements Gray—Albuquerque, New Mexico. When winter descends, the aroma of blueberries plucked from nature's bounty and bursting inside muffins as they bake in the oven carries Stott and Clare back to the cabin they love.

To feel what the Stotts feel, to inhale the fresh air they breath at their summer home, to swim with them in the cold, clear lake, to watch stars spread a canopy above them when darkness pushes the day away is to immerse yourself in *Wild Blueberry Summer*. The Introduction, the engaging chapters, the stunning photographs, and the Epilogue will draw you into a world far beyond the chaos of politics, racism, and social upheaval. As you turn each page, you'll become acquainted with flora and fauna, with a woodland thick with deciduous and pine trees, and with a way of life at the lake that is inclusive of the goodness residing in the animal and fowl kingdom and in mankind.

Enjoy this book and your spirits will be lifted as you, too, soar above the mundane, the anger, and the ugliness threatening to engulf us. Stott, as did his father, mastered the art of storytelling. He does not flaunt his intelligence, but skillfully weaves it throughout his well-written, descriptive stories that enchant readers, leaving them yearning for more. *Wild Blueberry Summer* does not disappoint. It invites you to walk with the author as he engages all your senses and makes you feel glad to be alive.

Lakeside Summers – How it Began

In 1985, Carol and I bought a cabin beside Crooked Lake in Michigan's Upper Peninsula. We called it the Little Cabin in the Big Woods. Since then, I, along with family members and close friends, have spent all or parts of extended summers at the cabin. Many of the special moments at the lake and the treasured memories these created, I celebrated in my 2022 book *Summers at the Lake: Upper Michigan Moments and Memories*. The book also included memories of the childhood summers spent decades earlier at Shawnigan Lake on Vancouver Island, Canada, as well as a few newspaper pieces my father, a columnist for *The Victoria Daily Times*, had written about those long-ago days.

Since *Summers at the Lake* was published in 2022, there have been more special moments at and around the Little Cabin in the Big Woods, and more incidents from days long-gone have surfaced from the deep well of memory. *Wild Blueberry Summer: More Upper Michigan Moments and Memories* includes short essays written during the summer of 2024, along with columns by my father, whose spirit, years after his death beside the Vancouver Island lake, has become my mentor and guide, helping me, by example, to find the words to express why a lifetime of summers at the lakes have become so special for me.

In the Preface to *Summers at the Lake*, I wrote that no two summers at the lake are the same, but that there is an underlying rhythm to all of them. Once again I have tried to evoke elements of this rhythm in individual pieces and in the order of presentation from the opening of camp as the leaves spring to life in mid-May to their beginning to turn red and gold in the waning days of summer. The moments and memories presented here are my father's and my own. But I hope that they will evoke for readers memories of similar incidents and feelings they have experienced at other lakes and at other times.

NOTE; The word "Anishinaabe," which occurs frequently in the following pages, is the name the Ojibwe (Chippewa) people of the Lake Superior region have long used to identify themselves.

Introduction - *Querencia*

> One achieves a slow, indelible intimacy with a place, learning to match its moods with one's own. At such times it is as if a destination had awaited us with nearly human expectation and with an exquisite blend of receptivity and detachment.
>
> Shirley Hazzard, *The Ancient Shore: Dispatches from Naples*

During the winter months I spend in Albuquerque, New Mexico, the "City of the Pavements Gray," I often find myself thinking about the Little Cabin in the Big Woods and my heart fills with the wonderful sensation of *querencia*.

Querencia is a Spanish term I learned just over a decade ago, shortly after I had moved to New Mexico. It comes from the verb *querer*, to want or desire, and refers to an intellectual, emotional, and spiritual love of a place—not just the physical landscape, but its history, the people and other beings who live there, and its spiritual quality.

Querencia is not a feeling I experienced four decades ago when we first entered the cabin and then walked down to the lake. It grew gradually—subtly and gently. Each year as we made the long drive, first from Western Canada and now from Albuquerque, the experience grew stronger. "Why don't you find somewhere closer to home?" people would ask us. We gave trite answers about the price of the place being right and about the terrain being suitable for our daughter Clare to easily move about in her wheelchair, not realizing that it was the growing power of *querencia* driving us.

Over the years, our feelings for our little half-acre of land fronting a small fishing lake, for the acres around it, for the nearby towns, and, indeed, for all of the Upper Peninsula grew. None of our experiences were spectacular; they just quietly became part of a growing feeling of *querencia*. The neighboring cabins were, like ours, simple: in the beginning some had no electricity, nor telephone, nor indoor plumbing. Their occupants were unpretentious, enjoying as we did the quiet but ever-changing scenes in the natural world that surrounded us.

We gradually discovered the myriad wonders of nature beside the lake: the flowers of the seasons from the tiny pussy-toes of spring to the purple asters of fading summer; the hummingbirds who came to our feeders; the does and their fawns who came timidly to the lake to drink by the dawn's early light; the loon chicks who made their first appearances clinging to a parent's back; the screeching morning calls of sandhill cranes; and the nighttime chorus of coyotes yipping from the darkened woods not far away.

We learned about the long past of Crooked Lake, where relics from early woodlands people have been discovered on the point across the water; where, in the middle of the nineteenth century, the surveyor William Burt created the first map of the area; and where weathered white pine stumps behind the cabin were reminders of the axe-wielding army of loggers that crossed the Upper Peninsula later in that century.

We spent most of our time around the cabin and on the lake, but regularly ventured abroad, getting to know and look forward to revisiting such places as the Sand Point Marsh Trail near Munising; Lakenland, the junkyard sculpture park near Marquette; and Marquette itself, walking past its historic buildings, buying reading supplies at a local book store, and enjoying open-faced whitefish sandwiches at the Vierling , where we gazed out the window at the gigantic ore dock stretching out into the lake.

We gradually developed warm friendships with Yoopers, permanent residents of the Upper Peninsula, the people who helped us every year: Norm, who transformed our barebones two-room, bathroom-free cabin into a comfortable second home; Brenda, who made sure delivery of the *Mining Journal*, a necessity for this newspaper-loving family, would start on the day after our arrival; and Sharon, a writer who encouraged me to share my scribbling with others. And especially Deb, a family friend of nearly half-a-century, who could take us on a forest walk of a few hundred yards and show us wonders that we would never have discovered ourselves. Her photographs have graced *Summers at the Lake* and grace this book.

Each year as spring gets closer and closer, I think about all of this, and then, to quote the English poet William Wordsworth, images of many places and people "flash upon that inward eye which is the bliss of solitude." And then my heart with *querencia* fills.

1 Winter in the City

One day in an Albuquerque parking lot, I noticed a car with a bumper sticker that read: "My heart is in the UP, but my butt is stuck here." It reflected what I often feel during fall and winter. For the first few months after I've left the Little Cabin in the Big Woods, I remember the events of the summer past. But then, in the new year, as the days lengthen, I start anticipating and planning for my return. Instead of being like a kid moping through the opening weeks of the school year, I become like one counting the weeks and then the "sleeps" until the big day arrives when I'll turn off Michigan Highway 94 and start driving down the dirt road to the place that had seemed long-ago and far away.

The Window and the Wall

The picture window above my desk in Albuquerque looks east to the Manzano Mountains. Often during the winter, I watch the changing predawn colors above the skyline and the gradual appearance of the silhouettes of the peaks. In the late afternoon, the sun shining from the west reveals foothills and valleys that had hidden themselves during most of the day. Today, the sky is gray above the Manzanos, but the hills are dusted with snow. It isn't much, but it will bring a little moisture to our drought-stricken land.

Unfortunately, the window also looks out on Eastern Avenue, which stretches from our house through what the locals call the "War Zone." Frequently, the predawn is illuminated by the flashing red and blue lights of police cars and other emergency vehicles. During the day, homeless people push their overburdened shopping carts along the edge of the road. It's not unusual to see a person walking down the middle of the street, waving arms wildly and carrying on a loud conversation with an unseen listener.

When the mountains are covered with clouds or the scene on Eastern is too much, I have a simple remedy. I turn my chair around and look at the wall. I'm not throwing in the towel or becoming a Stott-family version of Melville's catatonic character Bartleby, the Scrivener. I'm looking at three pictures Clare took of Crooked Lake. They're a Christmas gift, twenty by thirty inch enlargements forming a triptych of the lake taken from the dock on which I have spent so many golden hours.

The first picture looks south along the shore. In the foreground, the hemlock we call the Tom Thomson tree leans out over the water, tenaciously clinging to the bank as it has for decades. It was Carol's favorite tree. Along the south shore, the home of Joe Lakosky peeps through the willow trees. He's a year-around resident who grew up at the north end of the lake and, when he decided it was time to leave home, jumped in his boat and headed for a spot a mile away.

Hankie, our aussi-doodle, dominates the central picture. He's just come out of the lake, leaving pools of water on the weathered planks of the deck. He seems to be staring at something that isn't in the picture. In the distance, you can see the "Rooster Tree," a tall, spindly hemlock whose top looks like the silhouette of a barnyard fowl. It's the favorite resting place of a bald eagle who regularly visits us from his home in the Seney Wildlife Refuge, twenty miles away.

The third picture is a view of the lake facing east from the dock. A patch of morning sunlight brightens a few planks of the dock, the ripples sparkle, and the tops of the maples and birches across the lake catch the light of the young day. There are no boats or boat-wakes on the water. Jutting from the edge of the photograph is someone's arm. Perhaps it is Craig or Alberto or even me sitting on the loveseat, sipping coffee and absorbing the beautiful serenity.

As I gaze at the wall and the pictures that are windows to another place that is now far away, I smile and think that in a few months I'll be sitting on that dock, a part of the scene that's in the pictures Clare gave me for Christmas.

The (Blueberry) Muffin Man

On a Saturday morning, as a rare mid-February snow started to dust the City of the Pavements Gray, I lit a cheery blaze in the fireplace and started to make a batch of muffins to accompany the brunch Clare was preparing. I used the final cup of blueberries I'd picked last July in my secret berry patch not far from the Little Cabin in the Big Woods.

As I began the preparations, I started humming (softly – to spare the ears of Clare and the dogs) a song I'd learned long, long ago in grade school. It began "Do you know the muffin man?" As I blended the berries into the batter, I thought about what now seemed like a long ago day when I'd picked them.

Last summer had been the first time I'd picked berries since 2017. One season I'd arrived too late. The next year a family illness kept me in Albuquerque, and the year after that, it was the COVID epidemic. In 2021 and 2022, I'd had to leave the lake before there was even one ripe berry. Last summer, I knew I'd be around when the berry picking season arrived.

Two days before my scheduled departure, it began to rain—just a fine drizzle, what we used to call a "Scotch mist." It was warm and the mosquitoes were out in force. But, I slathered my hands with bug-juice, put on my beekeeper's hat, grabbed the plastic pail I'd been using for years, and drove to the two-track that led to my secret blueberry patch. The peak of the season was still a couple of weeks away, but there were berries, enough for at least four or five batches of muffins. They weren't plentiful; there were usually only a few on each branch. But, as the drizzle became a shower and the mosquitoes whined angrily in front of the mesh that covered my face, I ranged over a half acre. After a couple of hours, I was getting soaked, but the pail was over half full. It was time to go back to the cabin, sort the berries, picking out the wizened ones, the little twigs, and a few ants and then freeze the harvest.

A week later, back in Albuquerque, I made the first batch of wild blueberry muffins since 2017. We had another batch for Canadian Thanksgiving, then one for American Thanksgiving, and a big batch for Christmas morning. They were so good, their flavor enhanced by the memories of again picking after so many missed summers.

A ping from the oven announced that the muffins were done. I took them out of the oven, and we enjoyed them as we sat in front of the fire. In my head, I sang the concluding lines of the old song, but with variations: "Oh yes, I am the blueberry muffin man, the blueberry muffin man." I started thinking ahead to June, when I'd again start inspecting the blueberry patch, awaiting the time when I could pick the berries to bring back home, where I would once again become the muffin man—the blueberry muffin man.

On the Road Again

There's a tune that's been running through my head again and again over the last few days: Willie Nelson's "On the Road Again." I understand why. Soon, I'll begin the nearly two thousand mile drive to Crooked Lake. Like Willie, I "just can't wait to get on the road again."

Both Willie and I are anticipating our departures with joy. But the sources of our joy are quite different. First, Willie is looking forward to "makin' music with my friends." I'm not a music maker. I was encouraged to lip-sync during the school Christmas concerts long, long, ago. Willie is anticipating "Goin' places that I've never been/ Seein' things I may never see again." On the other hand, I'm going to a place I've been so many times before, a cherished destination that I've so often daydreamed of about during the long winter months.

And so, as I travel along the road, passing by the edge of the Black Hills, crossing the wide Missouri, gazing at the mighty Mississippi from the rest area on a Minnesota hillside, seeing Lambeau Field rising up on the eastern horizon as I pass through Green Bay, I'll be thinking of the friends I'll soon be rejoining.

I'll enjoy chatting with my fellow human snowbirds, catching up on winter activities and repeating old war stories. And, before they arrive, I'll be happy to be reunited with non-human friends—the tiny flowers that bloom in the spring, the green-yellow leaves that have burst from their green and copper colored buds, the solitary loon calling back to its mate on the nest, the hummingbird hovering just outside the screen porch waiting impatiently for me to fill the feeder.

And this year, I want to get to know my avian friends better. I'm going to learn about their journeys south and back again, about the spiritual and medicinal powers the native peoples found in them, the folktales that have been told about their lives in myth time.

The lake and its people (two and four legged) are old friends for whom familiarity does not breed contempt, but better understanding and deeper love. I'll be humming "On the Road Again" as I head east, but I'll be trying to create some new verses about the wonderful place that lies at the end of the journey.

Cross Over the Bridge

Fig 1-1: A mother turkey helps her offspring safely cross over a bridge.

Late one morning last week, as I crossed the Interstate Bridge that connects Marinette, Wisconsin to Menomonee, Michigan, I began smiling and humming a tune from my teenage years. I was smiling because midway across the bridge was a "Welcome to Michigan" sign. On the fifth day of my journey, I was getting closer to the Little Cabin in the Big Woods.

The song I hummed was Patti Page's 1954 hit "Cross over the Bridge." In it, the "Singing Rage" urged listeners (presumably male) to leave their fickle ways behind them so that true romance would find them. The song was picked up by a Seattle car dealership that urged listeners to their commercial to "cross over the bridge, Ballard Bridge." On the other side they'd discover great deals on new automobiles.

I wasn't humming because I was getting closer to true romance or because I wanted to buy a shiny new car. I'm too old to be following fickle ways that ought to be left behind, and my van, now ten years old, has only seventy thousand miles on it and should last its octogenarian owner until he's too old to be crossing bridges.

I was humming because what I was leaving behind: the City of the Pavements Gray, where the night noises were the sounds of gunshots, sometimes too close for comfort, and the wail of sirens coming from the not-too-distant district known as the War Zone. I was leaving a place where the morning newspaper, *The Journal*, filled too many of its constantly decreasing number of pages to stories of violent crimes, lurid trials, and international crises. Now, my night noises would be the sounds of breezes through the trees, the dogs whimpering in their sleep, and the occasional snap of a mousetrap. The local paper, also *The Journal*, would be delivered to the mailbox in the late morning. Its Friday edition might include a color photograph of a great blue heron, the story of a community's gathering to help neighbors who'd been left homeless after an apartment building fire, and a police log in which the most serious crimes were a man's standing in the street yelling and a dog barking incessantly after its owners had left it outside (and unleashed) when they'd gone to work.

As I drove along Michigan 35 and US 2 toward the cabin, I caught glimpses of Lake Michigan through the trees. And I thought about how each of the arrivals at my family's special place had involved crossing bridges before entering what I like to call "the home stretch." Nearly half-a-century ago, it was the Mackinac Bridge—simply the "Bridge," as we fondly call it. The very young kids, strapped into their car seats and either bored or sleepy from the six-hour trip from Kalamazoo, would perk up and crane their necks hoping to be the first to sight the towers rising up in the north. The bridge was then only fifteen-years-old, but it was already being called "iconic"—an automobile link between the Upper and Lower Peninsulas.

A few years later, it was a tiny bridge over the Montreal River that separated Hurley, Wisconsin, once a hell-town in the pines and still home to over two dozen bars along the main street, some of them featuring "Hollywood Dancers," and Ironwood, Michigan, a much more sedate town that celebrates its museums, an art gallery, and downtown parks. It was the third morning since we'd left our home in Edmonton in Western Canada, and our joy was not seeing advertisements for dancers, but knowing that, when we'd crossed the bridge into Ironwood, we'd only be half-a-day from the place we'd been dreaming about all through the long, dark, cold winter.

For a couple of years, we crossed from Canada to the Upper Peninsula on the International Bridge connecting the two Sault Ste

Maries—Ontario and Michigan. We'd glance down at the ships moving through the locks which, since the 1850s had linked the provinces and states of Lake Superior to the big cities of the American Midwest. It had only been a two-day drive from Connecticut to Crooked Lake, but our excitement was as great as ever.

And now, it's a four-and-a-half day journey from New Mexico to the UP. There was heavy traffic this year from Albuquerque to Santa Fe; long, boring stretches on two-lane back roads through the plains; and torrential rains and winds and nearby tornadoes in Wisconsin. I turned in early each night and got up slightly weary and steeled myself for the day's drive. But the fifth morning was different. The threatening storms had passed away, the traffic was light, and I eagerly began my drive. Three hours later, I arrived in Marinette and began to cross over the bridge.

And then, my heart with gladness filled, I began humming Patti Page's song, and I knew that I was crossing over the bridge to a life that was old and familiar, but ever new and fresh. Soon, I'd be pulling in the driveway far away from big cities, big crises, and the pressures these bring.

Leave your stressful days behind you and peace and joy will find you, to adapt Patti's words. And now that I've crossed over the bridge and will soon be at the Little Cabin in the Big Woods, I know that these words will come true.

2   May – Ever-Returning Spring

Hummingbirds, robins, and monarch butterflies are nearing the end of their long journeys to the Upper Peninsula while I'm packing and counting sleeps. Tiny flowering plants are coming to life beneath the carpet of brown leaves. The last snow banks are melting in the deep woods. The serviceberry bushes will soon blossom and, a couple of weeks later, their white petals will float to the ground, the last "snowfall" of early spring. The miracle of ever-returning spring has occurred. Soon my fellow human snowbirds and I will return to the lake we love.

Sharing the Land

Fig. 2-1: In a rare display of hospitality, the resident hummingbird shares his "dining table" with friends.

This morning, as I went to the woodshed in the gray pre-dawn to gather kindling and starter pieces for the fireplace, I heard two wonderful voices: a robin was singing in full-throated ease from a nearby tree, and a hummingbird whirred and chirped as he flew close to the screen porch to see if I'd refilled his feeder.

A few minutes later, as I sat in my aging recliner, watching the flames in the fireplace and then shifting my gaze toward the lake where the sun was beginning to gild the mist rising from the water, I saw the early morning songsters. The robin was perched on a sturdy branch of a tree, the hummingbird on a twig.

The robin was the first to leave his viewing post. He flitted to the ground where he hopped, stopped, and tilted his head as he searched for breakfast. Then the hummingbird returned to the feeder and, finding I'd fulfilled my refilling responsibilities, started lapping up the sugary liquid. I finished my coffee and headed to the table to consume my usual boring weekday breakfast: a generic brand of yogurt, ditto for honey-nut oat circles, and an unknown brand of cinnamon raisin bagels.

Later in the morning, as I was raking up last autumn's leaves, I thought about the similarities between me and my co-tenants, the robin and the hummingbird. Each of us was a biped, me being the only unfeathered one. We were all three snowbirds, two literal, one figurative. The robin may have spent his winter in the south-eastern states, perhaps Florida, like many of my fellow cabin owners. The hummingbird probably made the incredibly long journey across the Gulf of Mexico to Mexico and Central America. I drive five days to New Mexico. These avian wonders are always here at Lot 18 when I return to the Upper Peninsula in mid-to-late May. That's another thing we share—we always come back to the same spot.

The robin's aubade is not a celebration of the early morning but his way of establishing his territory. And the hummingbird is very defensive of the feeder, driving away others of his kind that dare to approach it. And I have frequently been heard referring to the Little Cabin in the Big Woods as MY place at the lake.

But the three of us, who by the way are male, are wrong. This little half-acre doesn't belong to any of us. Officially, it's the property of the United States Forest Service, a branch of the federal government, which has the right to tell me what I can or cannot do with the land. I'm allowed to do what I want inside the cabin, which I own, although over the years Carol and, later, Clare have decided on and overseen any interior decoration improvements.

Then I began to think: it's not just my two companions and I who don't own the land. In reality, the federal government doesn't either. It just thinks it does. Long before the Crooked Lake cabins were built, members of the early woodland tribes and their successors, the Anishinaabe, spent time here. Arrowheads and other discarded artifacts have been discovered on the little peninsula across the water from "my" place. They, too, were probably only summer residents, and, like me, they most likely harvested blueberries. And ancestors of the robin and the hummingbird certainly sought out earthworms and flower nectar.

The Anishinaabe respected the land and celebrated the life on it. In their own way, I'm sure, the ancestors of my co-tenants, the robins and hummingbirds, did too. It is a lesson I'm learning; each year my appreciation for the gift of being a tenant on this small piece of land on the eastern shore of Crooked Lake grows, and each year I understand more and more that there are responsibilities that come with the gift. I mustn't needlessly cut down trees and, if I have a campfire, I must not build it where there are overhanging limbs that could be killed by the rising heat. When I push the canoe into the water, I must be careful not to break the spiked iris "leaves" that have begun to rise from the bank. Only if I honor these and other responsibilities am I worthy of being a tenant.

Snakes Alive!

I take great pleasure sharing the land around the Little Cabin in the Big Woods with my co-tenants: the two snowbirds, squirrels and chipmunks, frogs, and other small creatures. Except for the hummingbird, who seems to confront me when I forget to fill his feeder, I don't interact with them. I leave them alone and enjoy watching them go about their daily activities.

I don't own the land, but I do own the cabin itself, and I object to the mice, the squatters who enter my house shortly after I depart in the fall and who are reluctant to leave when I return in the spring. If they insist on spending the winter months there, I wish that they would tidy up and exit the place before I turn into the driveway. They don't, and it's quite annoying.

We were tenant-free for the first three decades we'd been coming here. But in 2014, things changed for the worse. Clare and I had just arrived, and, when I began to fill the dogs' water dishes, three little gray faces appeared at the opening to the drainpipe. I grabbed a fly swatter, hit the mice, stunning them, and then tossed them into the woods.

I didn't tell Clare because I didn't want us to immediately start a long return journey to the City of the Pavements Gray. On our first trip to the store, I picked up three or four packages of mouse traps and a jar of Jiffy peanut butter—the creamy kind. "I noticed a couple of droppings," I told her. "Just in case there is a mouse inside, we better be prepared." Over the next several weeks, we were often awakened in the middle of the night by the snapping of the traps I'd bought.

It hasn't been that bad since that summer. But I always bring a fresh jar of Jiffy and some traps just in case.

When I discovered a couple of mice after I'd arrived this year at the Little Cabin in the Big Woods, I fixed the problem in a jiffy, you might say. Then, three days later, I discovered that there was another unwanted winter tenant. For the first couple of days, I'd only been using the microwave. But I decided to cook a real meal. And when I lit the gas stove—the right front burner and the oven—I was in for a big surprise.

I had gone to the cupboard to get some spices to stir into the concoction I was preparing for dinner. When I turned back to the stove, an eighteen-inch garter snake was slithering across the unlit back burners. He must have set up residence in the broiler drawer and had a hot awakening from his long winter's nap. I yelled out in surprise—not "Sakes Alive!" or even "Snakes Alive!"—but an utterance that would have got me sent to the principal's office if I'd said it when I was a schoolboy. I had the presence of mind to turn off the burner under the pot and, using the four-foot yardstick the local hardware store had given away as a promotion, herded the unwanted squatter to the back door.

I returned to the stove, turned on the burner, stirred in the spices, and finished cooking dinner. Then I sat down to unwind. "The Snake," by D. H. Lawrence, a poem we'd studied in my freshman English class, came to my mind. After his confrontation with the title character, the poet wrote, "I felt honoured ... that he should seek my hospitality."

Not me! If I'm going to have unwanted squatters wintering in my house, I'll take mice over snakes anytime!

Hospitality? Bah!

Rake's Progress

I'm usually back in the City of the Pavements Gray by mid-September and I miss the vivid gold and scarlet of the autumn leaves at Crooked Lake. But when I return in May, I find last autumn's leaves waiting for me, brown and sodden on the ground surrounding the Little Cabin in the Big Woods. So, one of the first major outdoor jobs of the season is to get out the rakes and wheelbarrow and start tidying things up.

Around noon yesterday, as I was leaning on my rake observing the (very little) progress I'd made on the area right around the cabin, a neighbor stopped to chat. Noticing my primitive tools, he asked if I'd like to borrow his power weed-whacker and blower. "You can do your whole lot in an afternoon," he told me. I declined politely, telling him that I was just about finished—I wasn't—but assured him that I'd take him up on his offer next year.

I was being polite. The day before, he'd been using his power equipment to clear leaves. It was loud and noisy. Then, after he'd made a big pile, he had poured lighter fluid on it and set the mound on fire. At least with my rake and wheelbarrow, I could hear the birds chirping and I could compost the leaves instead of incinerating them, making the air smell foul, and running the danger of an errant spark causing a bigger fire.

I had, however, a more important reason for using simple tools. In addition to the leaves covering the ground, there were clumps of spring's first flowers: bouquets of tiny little blossoms rising up to announce that the long winter was over and that they were the advance party, preparing the way for the bigger flowers of later spring, summer, and early autumn. There were purple gay-wings looking like little orchids, star flowers whose white petals were miniature versions of the lilies that would soon be blooming on the lake, yellow violets I wanted to hold under my chin to see if I liked butter, and strawberry blossoms that foretold a small but delicious crop of the finger-nail-sized fruits we prized every year.

Most important, there were bunches of forget-me-nots, their miniscule pale blue petals a reminder of Carol, who had asked me long ago to rake around the first clump that had appeared beside the back step. They won't fade like the other tiny blessings. They'll be around until at least mid-summer, reminding me of times long past, evoking a melancholically sweetness.

There is one spot, about five feet square that I won't rake at all. That's the place where, late in May or early in June, a lady slipper, the only one on the lot, blooms. The first tall flower of the year, it's a bashful plant, its flower hanging down like the tallest kid in the class, embarrassed around his shorter friends. The flower book says it's pink. But it's not a Barbie pink, demanding that everyone pay attention, but a dusky pink, inviting those who do take the time to notice to enjoy the few days it's around and to rejoice in its promise of bigger, brighter flowers to come.

And so, don't anticipate seeing me at Denman's' or Madigan's hardware stores in Munising during the late summer clearance sales. I don't want and I don't need a blower, a power weed-wacker, or a can of charcoal lighter. I'll still have a rake and wheelbarrow, and that's all I need for the simple and quiet activity of raking leaves, listening to the birds, and spying the tiny flowers.

At Last ... An Answer

One of the wonderful things about coming to the Little Cabin in the Big Woods is that you're constantly learning new things—about the cabin itself, the woods around, and the lake we canoe on and swim in. This morning I learned the reason for an event that occurred thirty-five years ago.

It happened on a Friday morning. Around midnight the night before, I had returned from Sault Ste Marie, Ontario where, twice a week I was teaching an English class at the local college. I wouldn't be making the two-hour (each way) trip until the next Tuesday, and so I celebrated the end of the work week with a mini-pizza and a couple of beers. I went to bed looking forward to sleeping in, waking up gradually, and spending the morning savoring the joys of lethargy.

But it wasn't to be. Just before sunrise, I was awakened by a loud metallic clanging. The old windup alarm clock said it was twenty minutes after six. I sprang from my bed to see what was the matter. Everything seemed all right in the cabin. However, the metal stovepipe extending to the roof from the space heater was reverberating from the noises. I pulled on my sweatpants and shirt, slathered my hands with bug juice, donned my beekeeper's hat with the mesh face covering, and stepped tentatively outside.

I looked up at the stovepipe and there was a woodpecker (don't ask me what kind—it was very early and I wasn't fully awake). It was standing on the roof, banging away noisily at the metal, only pausing briefly when I hurled some imprecations (none of them polite) at him. Then I very lightly tossed a pine cone on to the roof; it rolled down and when it touched the bird's legs, it flew away. I didn't see or hear it again on my roof, although a week later I thought I heard its pecking from a cabin a few lots away.

Over the summer, I related my experience to any of the neighbors who would listen. Most people remarked that it was very strange. One suggested it was the bird's method of sharpening and cleaning its bill. A couple looked at me as if I'd had more than two beers on that thirsty Thursday night. And so, the event remained a mystery, a one-time experience without an explanation.

Until this morning, thirty-five years later.

I was listening to National Public Radio's "Morning Edition." The news and a couple of serious features were over, and Sasha Pfeiffer, one of the regular contributors, began recounting an unusual event that had occurred in her house. She'd heard a loud metallic bagging and had checked the house before going outside, where she discovered a woodpecker working on a metal chimney.

When that had happened to me, I merely made casual, unsuccessful inquiries of a few neighbors. Sasha Pfeiffer did much better: she contacted a number of experts and found out that the bird's metallic peckings were meant to establish its territory and attract a mate to it.

Now I know what the racket was all about and why it wasn't repeated. The incredibly rude awakening hadn't achieved its intended purpose. The woodpecker found that this territory was unsuitable and that his call hadn't solicited any avian responses. I'm glad. I like to wake up when I want to.

If only the mice who sneak in would get the same message. During the summer, the Little Cabin in the Big Woods is not a suitable territory for them to defend or to raise a family in. Because of them, I occasionally get awakened before dawn—with the snapping of a mousetrap.

The 24th of May

This morning, when I drove into town on my weekly grocery run, the traffic on M-28 was heavier than usual. The parking lot at the supermarket was nearly full, and, when I arrived at the checkout stands, there were long lines at each station. I wasn't surprised: it was the Friday before the Memorial Day long weekend, before what is often called "the unofficial beginning of summer."

On the way home, the announcer preceded the noon news with the statement: It's Friday, May 24th. Hearing the date triggered memories. My mind drifted back to the late 1940s and early 1950s to the family lake place on Vancouver Island, British Columbia.

The 24th of May was our "unofficial beginning of summer." Sure we'd spent the Easter weekend there. But the weather was chilly and damp, the inside of the uninsulated cabin was very cold at night, and, except for the fact that on Sunday morning we'd harvest as many chocolate eggs, rabbits, and chicks as we could and then quickly devour them, we'd have been just as happy staying in town.

In those days, the 24th, officially called "Victoria Day," to honor the birthday of the nineteenth-century queen after whom our hometown was named, was actually observed on the 24th, not on a Monday to make it part of a long weekend. That meant that often the holiday fell on Tuesday, Wednesday, or Thursday. We loved that; it meant that we'd actually be at the lake in the middle of the week. There would be no homework or piano practice or trudging to and from Margaret Jenkins School, an incredibly long three blocks from home.

At three o'clock on the afternoon before the holiday, we'd race home from school, covering those three blocks in record time. There was no dilly dallying, talking with pals, or stopping at the corner store for a penny popsicle (made on the premises). We'd quickly change from our school clothes and pile into the 1939 Plymouth, which my mother had already packed with groceries, a precooked supper, extra clothes, clean sheets—and our bathing suits. We'd pick up my father at the newspaper office, and he'd drive the rest of the way. There was no stopping for a beer at the Six-Mile House or ice cream at the Malahat Chalet. We all wanted to get to the lake. One time, I remember my mother telling my father to slow down; he was going three miles over the 45 miles-per-hour speed limit.

After we'd trudged the hundred or so feet from the parking lot to the cabin, lugging incredibly heavy bags of clothing and groceries and then spent an excruciatingly long half hour unpacking the bags and making the beds (my sisters' jobs) and chopping stove-sized pieces of wood and lugging buckets of water up from the lake (my jobs), it was time the first swim of the year. My father sipped a lukewarm beer as he life-guarded us.

The 24th of May was wonderful—the best midweek day of the school year. It was, in the memory of this octogenarian, always sunny and warm and the mosquitoes were never present. My father cooked bacon and eggs for breakfast, a wonderful change from the shredded wheat and white toast of most weekday mornings. Our parents mercifully kept our chores to a minimum. We spent the rest of the day paddling around in kayaks, splashing each other as we waded into the water, and warming up and drying off lying on an old army blanket spread on the rough ground. Alas, we spent far too much time in the sun, and we weren't slathered with sun-block, which virtually nobody had heard of in those days.

During the afternoon, we often wished the day would never end. But after dinner, we wanted to get back to town and willingly cleaned up and packed up the car. We had to be back in Victoria and settled in before nine-o'clock. That's when the fireworks display, which we could view from our parents' bedroom window, began.

The next day we reported back to school tired and sunburned. And, if it was a Thursday, things were even worse. That's the day I had my piano lessons, and I'd missed practice on both the 23rd and 24th. I'd be in for a scolding. But it was worth it for the times that we'd had.

If there ever were such things as halcyon days, those long-ago weekday celebrations of 24th of May, the unofficial first day of summer, would certainly be included. I wouldn't trade them for a whole bunch of Monday holidays.

The First Dip

"Last one in's a rotten egg!"

That's the challenge that the kids used to issue when, long, long ago, we prepared to take the initial dip of the season at Shawnigan Lake. My sisters and my cousin Mike, who were pretty hard-boiled, always dove in first. My cousin Wendy and I, who were quite timid, often tied for the title of rotten egg.

Fig. 2-2: After a long nap on my bed, Hankie (left) and Katrina decide to become life guards when I take my first dip

Here in the UP, I don't have to worry about being given the title. It's not that I've become hardboiled; it's just that I usually arrive at the Little Cabin in the Big Woods alone and before people have come to the other cabins. The first dip generally occurs between the last few days of May and the first few of June. Once, when my son and I stopped at the cabin on the way east, it happened on the last day of April. I was much younger then, it was an unseasonably warm day, and both of us had some antifreeze in our blood.

This year, I took my first dip on May 24, the same day my cousins, my sisters, and I used to make our first test of the waters at Shawnigan. This wasn't on the first day of my arrival, which has usually been the case. On Tuesday, I'd been too tired after the long trip; on Wednesday, it was raining; and on Thursday, the air temperature had hovered in the lower 50s. On Friday, conditions weren't that much better, but I decided to quit procrastinating. It was time to take the plunge.

But not before some careful planning. My first dip in Crooked Lake is always a ceremonial occasion, and there are certain ritual steps that had to be taken. First, I went down to the lake to check the water temperature. It was just under 65 (on the surface), acceptable for a quick dip, but not a real swim. Then, it being a cloudy and cool day, I lit the fire and made sure it was burning steadily. I changed into my very old, faded, and baggy bathing suit. I didn't need to dress up; after all there would be no witnesses to this momentous event. Then I slathered myself with mosquito lotion to make sure that, as I ran the twenty yards from the cabin to the shore, I wouldn't be carried away by bloodthirsty members of the Upper Peninsula Air Force. I slowed down as I reached the water's edge, but, knowing that he who hesitates is lost (or kidnapped by the nasty little insects), I waded quickly in until I reached waist-deep water.

The water was brisk, the air colder, and the mosquitoes were gathering. I turned toward the shore, plunged underwater, took two strokes, surfaced and then took three more. When the water became too shallow, I stood up, waded the last two steps to the shore, grabbed my towel, raced to the cabin, and dried myself off as I stood before the fire. I got into my clothes and now, toasty warm, decided to toast the occasion. I popped open a bottle of Bell's Oberon, a wheat beer that has a drawing of a stylized sun on the label and is described as being "like sunshine in a glass."

It started to rain outside, but I was dry and happy. Once again, I wasn't the rotten egg. And I remembered a time long ago, when I'd stood in front of the fire in preparation for being the first in the water that year. I had made up my mind that no matter how cold the weather or the water, I was determined to do it. The date was December 31. We were celebrating New Years Eve at Shawnigan Lake, and I'd announced my intention to my smirking sisters. "I'm going to be the last in during the old year and the first in in the new." At 11: 59: 40 p.m. I waded in and made it up to my waist when I felt my legs cramping and instantly decided to rush back to shore, where my father, who was shining a flashlight on his watch, told me: "It's 11:59: 55."

By the time I got inside, it was past midnight. One of my sisters, still smirking, remarked: "Better luck next year."

A Three Dog Night ... Almost

On Friday morning, the man on the radio had proclaimed that coming weekend would mark the "unofficial beginning of summer." But Saturday and Sunday, the temperatures were five or so degrees below normal. Thankfully there was no rain and just enough of a northerly breeze to keep the mosquitoes down to an (almost) manage-able number. At the campground, kids in down-filled jackets were riding their bikes along the road, most adults were huddled around campfires, and a few hardy fishermen stood on the banks or rowed boats into the lake to try their luck. Here at our lake, I was able to work around the yard, listen to the sounds of my neighbors doing the same, and, in the late afternoon, enjoy a beer while sitting at the dock (wearing my down-filled vest).

That changed on Monday, Memorial Day. Just after dawn, the rain started and the north wind became stronger. The rain didn't stop for eight hours and when it did, the mosquitoes returned with a vengeance. Checkout time at the Colwell Lake campground was supposed to be at noon. But when I drove by just before ten o'clock, most sites were empty and, in others, people were rapidly picking up, packing, and preparing to depart.

The next two-and-a-half days were acceptable—cooler than usual but dry, and with just enough of a north wind to hinder the blood-thirsty activities of the Upper Peninsula's Air Force. But the local evening news brought bad tidings: temperatures would plunge to the mid-thirties during the night. I feared for the blueberries when I heard that in places there would be killer frosts.

At bedtime, I donned my long-johns instead of my usual pajamas and put an extra blanket on the bed. When I woke up, as I usually do, in the wee small hours, I felt particularly warm. I quickly discovered why. Hankie, the fifty pound aussi-doodle, and Katrina, the eighty pound Maremma, an Italian cousin of a Pyrenees, had taken over most of the bed. Maremmas are supposed to be hardy outdoor dogs, but not Katrina. She pushed against me for warmth, and I found myself clinging to the edge of the bed.

Before I returned to the bedroom, I turned on the baseboard heaters. They're not incredibly efficient, but they do take the chill off, and they certainly increase profits for the shareholders of the power company. When I approached the bed, I discovered the dogs had stretched out and were taking nearly all the space. My stern words weren't enough to budge them, and so I had to go to the kitchen and vigorously shake the jar containing the dog treats. They responded quickly and as they chewed their midnight snacks, I rushed to the bed and re-staked my (meager) claim.

In the early morning, the indoor-outdoor thermometer read 36 degrees. I lit a cheery fire, made my morning coffee, and gazed out the window watching mist rise from the lake. The dogs settled comfortably in front of the fire. The pictures of the dogs lounging happily, the flames flickering warmly, and the mist being illuminated by the rays of the rising sun brought joy to my heart. But it also brought a tinge of anxiety. I wondered how the blueberry bushes had survived. They didn't have the benefit of two large bed-hogging canines to help them through the three-dog night.

The Silence of the Loons

Fig. 2-3: Of all the families on the lake, human or animal, the loons are the most revered. Joy greets their annual early spring return.

"The call of a loon at night is the loneliest sound I've ever heard," a city-dwelling friend once said to me. I disagreed silently. When a loon's cry echoes across the lake at night, it means that there's communication with another loon, most often a spouse. The call may be a warning of danger, an aggressive challenge to intruders, expressions of happiness or curiosity, or just quick helloes to a mate back on the nest.

And so, when I hear a call of a loon, I'm not sad or lonely, but happy. What does make me sad is when there are no calls. I thought of this in the winter when a friend sent a post about a famous loon and again shortly after I'd arrived at the Little Cabin in the Big Woods.

The post was about ABJ, the most famous and probably the oldest loon in the world. In 1987, just two years after we had bought the cabin, he was hatched and banded at the Seney Wildlife Refuge. At the time of my last visit to the Refuge, six years ago, he was still happily married to Fe, whom he'd been with since 1997. They'd raised many chicks over the years and were now grandparents, with the oldest grandchild well into her teens.

Then, a couple of years ago, shocking news reached ABJ's many human friends. Fe, realizing that he was, so to speak, no longer the diver he used to be, had dumped him for a younger fellow. She had become a kind of avian cougar. Not to be outdone, the jilted old fellow found a younger chick, and for a couple of summers all was well. But now, she, too, has moved on, and he swims alone and silent.

This spring, I had neither seen nor heard any loons on Crooked Lake during the first two weeks after my arrival. Over several summers, I'd come to see the pair that summered there as fellow snow-birds, returning each year to the same lake, as loons do. Then, one afternoon, as I sat at the dock, I thought I saw one loon swimming far out from shore. "Wonderful," I exclaimed to myself. "They're back!" I figured that the other loon was on the nest and that soon they'd all be swimming along in a family outing.

But my happiness was quickly crushed. As the bird came closer, I noticed that it wasn't diving the way a loon does. It swam lower in the water and it didn't have a speckled necklace. It was a cormorant, a member of an invasive species, one that not only depletes the fish stock of a lake, but also often drives off and kills competitors.

Had this bird driven off or killed my summer neighbors, or have the loons met their ends elsewhere? Perhaps one had left the other for a more a more attractive partner. The silence of the night now brings with it a note of sadness.

Treasured Old Clothes

When I arrived at the Little Cabin in the Big Woods, I'd been on the road for four-and-a half days and was really tired. So when I unpacked, I haphazardly hung shirts and pants on hangers in the closet, piled T-shirts on the cupboard shelves, and stuffed socks and underwear into drawers. It was all a bit of a hodgepodge, and each morning, it took longer than usual to find appropriate clothes.

I needed to do something, not only for my own convenience, but also because Clare would be arriving in a couple of weeks. As she inspected the rooms in the house, she'd look at my closet, cupboard, and drawers and say, "What a mess! How do you ever find anything? Don't you ever throw anything away?" And so, early this afternoon, when a few drops of rain caused me to drop my rake and rush indoors, I decided it was time to sort and, if necessary, throw away.

In half-an-hour, the garments in the closet and on the cupboard shelves had been divided into two groups: the clothes I'd wear if I were travelling, going to a library, or walking down the lakeside path to enjoy dinner at a neighbors' place, and clothes that were a little frayed at the collars and cuffs or thin at the knees but were certainly good enough for when I was alone pretending to finish the multitudinous chores both in the house and outside. In the days of long ago, we would have called those in the first group our "school clothes" and those in the second, our "play clothes."

In a large garbage bag on the bed were clothes that were so old that they needed to be consigned to the rag bag or left at the dump. Beside the bag was a small pile of clothes that were also very old, but that I couldn't part with. Each evoked so many memories, some of them about my youth and some about special people who are no longer with us. When I look at them or sometimes even wear them, I get misty eyed.

The two oldest items are from the late 1950s. One is a cruiser's vest, a khaki sleeveless jacket with lots of pockets, which I wore when I was a (very unimportant) member of a British Columbia Forest Service survey crew. I wear it when I bicycle out to the highway to get the paper and, as I pedal through the woods, I think of the wonderful summers of so long ago. The second is a Black Watch tartan shirt my mother had bought for me when I left for university in Vancouver. Clare wears it now when we go down to the dock on cool and breezy summer evenings, and, when we do, she often asks me questions about her grandmother.

There are two sweatshirts from the 1980s. One, which has red and white striped sleeves and a blue body, was a Christmas gift from Sheri, my twin sister. Somebody once said that it looks like a flag in heat, but when I wear it on cool evenings, I think of her great, good heart. The other is a heavy gray sweatshirt that Carol bought especially to bring to the cabin. It is well over three decades old, but it does a wonderful job of warming me, body and soul, when I put it on in the early mornings.

There are two t-shirts bearing the logos of defunct athletic teams. One is of the Duluth-Superior Dukes, who played in one of my favorite old stadiums, "The Wade" of Duluth, Minnesota. The other is of the

Memphis Maniax of the ill-fated X (as in extreme) FL. It was a Christmas gift from one of my favorite nephews (Sheri's son). Neither the Dukes nor the Maniax are around any longer, but the T-shirts have lasted and are still in pretty good shape. When I wear them I'm reminded of fun games I'd watched, either in person or on TV and, in the case of the XFL one, of a really nice kid (now a father of two wonderful girls).

And finally, there's a pair of black slip-on shoes, which were called loafers at the shoe-store, but really look like the "space-shoes" worn by dowdy-looking trainers at the Westminster Dog Show. I used to wear them for teaching, but one day a new puppy in the house discovered them in a closet I'd forgotten to shut. The local shoemaker couldn't repair the gnawed flap at the top of one of them. But, they were still in good shape and so, come the summer, I brought them to the lake. I still wear them and when I do, I think of Zoe, a wonderful rescue dog and a close companion for so many years.

I don't want these clothes to get any more worn than they are, so I don them sparingly. They are important items in what I call my Museum of Historical Garments.

3   June – Bustin' Out All Over

Although signs of spring abound in May, there are times when people wonder if they're witnessing a false spring. Temperatures can plunge; there might even be an occasional snowflake in the air. But in June spring flourishes—tall, bright flowers rise toward the sky; a loon chick appears riding on its mother's back; in the morning more fishermen try their luck on the lake. It stays light until after ten o'clock. "Summer is icumen in."

Unofficial Summer Begins

They call Memorial Day the unofficial beginning of summer. But this year it rained most of the that day, and, during the rest of the following week, there were plenty of clouds, cold winds from the north, dawn temperatures below 40 degrees, and legions of mosquitoes. Then a week after the holiday, things changed almost overnight. It seemed that June was busting out all over.

When I came into the kitchen early Sunday morning, I noticed that, for the first time, none of the mouse traps had been sprung. The temperature inside the cabin was 61 degrees, so I didn't need to start a fire to drive off a chill. As I was sipping my coffee, I watched a man paddling a canoe in the calm and bright waters. Above him, the sun shone brightly. When the dogs went out for their morning walk, they weren't in danger of being carried away by mosquitoes.

It was just the kind of day I needed to finish cleaning away the leaves from around the cabin. The job should have been over with several days ago, but I'd made plenty of excuses for not doing so. All of them could be summed up in one word: lethargy. Today, the work was a pleasure—a warm breeze from the south kept the Upper Peninsula legions away. By the late afternoon, the job wasn't finished.

But, seeing the expanding areas of green that had previously been made dull brown by fallen leaves gave me a sense that the place was being transformed into something fresh and vibrant.

It was time to head down to the shore. Except for a few very brief dips I'd taken in the brisk water, I hadn't spent much time there since my arrival. This afternoon, the old water thermometer that now floats on the top said the surface temperature was 70 degrees. So, after I'd waded in up to my neck, molested along the way by only one mosquito, I swam a couple of dozen yards, did some duck dives, then, facing the shore, floated on my back gazing at the green pine trees with the blue sky above them.

The best was yet to come.

I dressed and headed to the dock with the dogs, the first time I'd been able to sit there this year. Even when the sun went behind the only cloud in the sky, it was warm. A gentle breeze from the southwest kept the mosquitoes away. I sipped a beer I'd picked up from LaTulip, a brewery less than an hour away. It was a light American lager called "Logger" and was clean, crisp, and refreshing, one of the best examples of the style I've tasted.

There was no one on the lake, no human voices from cabins along the shore, and no traffic noise from the highway beyond the trees. A squirrel scolded and a woodpecker drummed out a tattoo from the far side of the water. A fish splashed as it leapt into the air trying to catch dinner. In the reeds beside the dock, two frogs conducted a dialogue that would have made Aristophanes proud. Behind the cabin, the local songbirds began rehearsing their nightly vespers.

In the middle of the lake, a loon floated deep in the water, then disappeared below the surface in search of its dinner. It was the first time I'd seen a loon this year and, having feared the worst for two weeks, I was delighted. That he or she was alone filled me with joy. It meant that somewhere along the edge of the lake, its spouse was protecting the nest and waiting its turn to go out for dinner. When summer began, the chicks would, if all went well, be swimming beside their parents.

A few dozen yards from the dock, there were more signs of the approaching summer. Reeds that weren't there when I looked a couple of days ago were now poking several inches above the surface.

A late dinner over, the dishes washed, the dogs taken for the final stroll, I returned to the dock to watch the sun set. It still had a ways to go before it reached its northern terminus and set between the two towering white pines. But the vivid colors it painted the sky before it disappeared below the tree line were a reminder that there would be more end-of-the day splendors in the summer that would arrive in less than three weeks.

As we used to say when we were kids, "The sun has gone to bed." It was time for me to turn in as well. The outside temperature was well above sixty, so I decided that, for the first time this season, it would be safe to open the bedroom window. When I did, there were no mosquitoes buzzing at the screen. As I drifted off to sleep, I thought to myself, "If I were awakened in the middle of the night by one of the loons calling the other, I wouldn't be annoyed." I'd be very happy. It would be the perfect ending to what was for me the first unofficial day of summer.

The Blues in June

Fig. 3-1: The wild iris that bloom along the bank bring joy, even on gray days

This morning the air was clear and the lake, calm. I paddled the canoe along the shores, noticing here and there blue kayaks hauled up on the bank—signs of the recent arrival of other summer residents. As the sun rose higher, the sky became azure.

My short excursion over, I tied up the canoe. I noticed that the green spears of the iris plants were thrusting up from the bank. Soon the glorious blue and yellow flowers will grace the shoreline.

In the grass beside the path leading to the cabin, a robin hopped along, cocked its head, harvested a worm and flew to the nest to feed its hatchlings, recently-born from their fragile blue eggs.

Later that morning, I drove to my secret blueberry patch. The young fruit was still a pale pinkish color and many of the berries still had the star-shaped crowns, reminders of the fact that in the long-ago time, the Great Spirit had sent stars to earth, where, transformed into blue-berries, they fed starving children. When "my" blueberries are ripe, I'll freeze much of my harvest and take them to the City of the Pavements Gray and there make muffins as gifts for friends.

After my late afternoon swim, I noticed, beside the backdoor, a clump of powder-blue forget-me-nots that reminded me of long ago happy times.

As my dinner of leftovers warmed in the microwave, I sipped a "Beau Blue," a delightfully subtle, sweet and tart beer made at Barrel + Beam, a Marquette brewery that creates some wonderfully different beers.

During my short evening walk, I passed a blue spruce sapling with cards hanging on it. The tree and the cards celebrate the memory of mother and brother who had loved the lake.

Did I feel the blues today?

Yes—and with great joy.

Diary of a Rainy Week

Long ago, on the day before we headed to Shawnigan Lake for our annual summer vacation, my father used to write a humorous column lamenting that, because he had made a long list of outdoor chores and activities, it was likely to rain. "You may put away your garden sprinklers, good people. 'Sunspot' Stott is on the annual rainmaking expedition that passes for his vacation," he wrote one time. In another, he referred himself as "Chief Rainmaker" and noted that his name around the office was "He-Who-Brings-The-Rain." He once lamented, "I'm used to wet vacations."

I thought about his comments last Sunday, as I sat on the dock enjoying an unseasonably warm day. I'd been tired from the long drive from the City of the Pavements Gray and, for several days after my arrival had been suffering from frequent bouts of lethargy. Filled with guilt, I made the firm promise to myself that I'd finish cleaning up last autumn's leaves and winter's broken branches.

Tomorrow.

But when "tomorrow" arrived, so did the rains, and they returned several days during the week. And so, confined inside, I kept a diary about the wet week that followed the unofficial opening of summer at the lake.

Monday, 5.45 p.m.: The guy who wrote the song that included the line, "Sunshine always follows the rain" had it backward. Yesterday was wonderful. Today was cloudy, with the temperatures fifteen degrees colder. The mosquitoes were back at full-strength. As soon as I got my rakes out of the shed, the rain began. So, I decided that instead of raking, I'd vacuum the rugs; instead of swimming, I'd take a shower (I needed one); instead of sitting on the dock, I'd light a fire and sit in my comfortable lazyboy. Who says old men are stubborn and inflexible?

Tuesday, 9:39 a.m.: As I was walking the dogs, I felt the first drops of rain and by the time I got back to the cabin, the drops had turned into a deluge. It rained for the next six hours. The sun came out for a couple of hours, but by the evening, the clouds returned, along with thunder and lightning. Katrina, trembling with fear, turned herself into an eighty-pound lapdog.

Wednesday: I planned to rake until the job was done, but as I was leaning on the rake, looking out at the water, I noticed dimples on the surface of the lake. They weren't made by feeding fish. In a few minutes, the rains had returned in full force and I rushed inside.

Thursday: How do you know when it's going to rain? The roofer's truck arrives next door and, within a few minutes, a deluge forces the men retreat to their vehicle and return to town.

Friday: The wind from the north began to pick up in mid-morning and the temperature dropped below 50 degrees by noon. It didn't rain and the wind kept the mosquitoes down. So I got some raking done before I experienced another attack of lethargy.

Saturday: The temperature in the City of the Pavements Gray is 103 degrees and nobody wants to go outside. The temperature at the lake is 48 degrees and nobody wants to go outside.

Sunday: Same old, same old: clouds, followed by rain, followed by sunshine, followed by rain. The roofers left at noon. I vacuumed the rest of the house. And once again, I celebrated happy hour in front of a cheerful, warming fire.

I'm not sure, but I think I've inherited my father's title, or at least the role of "Son-of-He-Who-Brings-Rain." There are still a lot of leaves to rake up, but the inside of the Little Cabin in the Big Woods is as clean as it's been for quite a while. There's still more to do. Maybe I should make a commitment to finish the inside work during the coming week. Perhaps that would make the rain stop.

The Dawn's Early Light

The morning chorus of the birds streams through the window. The trees just beyond the window are silhouettes in the predawn light. The luminous hands on the old, windup alarm read 5:05 a.m. It's time to rise, shine, and greet the new day.

The temperatures on the thermometer on the living room wall reads 56 inside and 46 out. So, after I let Hankie out, I gather kindling and starter logs from the screened porch and start the fire. A lone mosquito that has followed me inside buzzes around my right ear (the good one). I quickly settle that problem.

Fig. 3-2: The shy lady slipper, the first of the taller plants to blossom, is the harbinger of the brightly-colored flowers to come.

The fire needs a little poking to encourage the flames. The coffee hasn't finished its brewing cycle, but it smells so good that I pour a cup, sit in my lazyboy and am about to take a first sip when Hankie scratches at the door. I let him in, take my first sip, and gaze at the fire and out the window.

It's 5:54 a.m., the official time for sunrise. Mist rises from the lake, a thin line of yellow gold light appears along the tops of the maples, birches, and alders across the water. Over the next half hour, the band of light widens as it travels down the trees toward the shoreline. The mist thins, dissipates, and then vanishes. A slight early morning breeze ripples the surface of the water. The gray in the sky is gradually transmuted into blue. The temperature inside has risen to 62; outside it is slowly creeping toward 50.

I've just put another log on the fire, when the door from the kitchen to the back of the house creaks. Katrina, the Maremma and the late sleeper of the family, has decided to join us. She noses the door open, stretches mightily, wags her tail lazily, ambles over to the outside door and scratches it. I get up and open it for her and then pour another cup of coffee. Just as I'm about to sit down, take another first sip and resume my gazing, Katrina scratches to be let in. She takes a drink of water, goes to the door leading to the screened porch and scratches again. I let her out; she hops up on to the very old couch and sits surveying the woods and the water. Hankie soon joins her.

By seven o'clock, it's completely light. My snowbird co-tenants are ready for breakfast: the hummingbird arrives at the feeder; the robin hops along searching for an earthworm. I begin to feel hungry myself, bring out the fry pan and start frying bacon. The dogs on the porch thrust their noses high into the air, sniffing vigorously. Then they get off the couch, walk to the door, and scratch it.

Half-an-hour later, breakfast is over. The dogs have each enjoyed a small piece of bacon and a bit of toast (buttered of course). They stretch out and snooze as I wash, dry, and put away the dishes. While I'm dressing, I hear several woofs followed by a cacophony of barks. The dogs are telling me that the roofers have arrived next door and are beginning their day's labor.

I glance at my to-do-today list; there are a lot of outside jobs on it. I slather bug dope on my hands and neck, put on my mesh-covered hat, and head outside, accompanied by my two canine non-helpers. As Michigan poet, the late Theodore Roethke, wrote in his poem "Bring the Day," "It is time to begin! To begin!"

Hockey Night in the Big Woods

Like most Canadians, I watch hockey loud, very loud—always have and probably always will. There are goals of the favorite team to be cheered for, mean plays by the opponents to be loudly booed, and obvious mistakes by the referees to be vociferously criticized.

It's all part of being a fan. But, sometimes, it can create awkward moments.

Over six decades ago, when Carol and I were living in an apartment, the season's opening telecast of *Hockey Night in Canada* occurred on an unseasonably warm Saturday evening. There was no air conditioning in the apartment and all the windows were open. I was excited that my favorite sport had returned and gave full vent to my cheers, boos, and criticisms, along with some pretty loud gasps and "ooohs." When the Maple Leafs scored the go-ahead goal late in the second period, the decibel level of my roar of approval was quite high. We heard the windows of the apartment above us bang shut.

A couple of days later, we were talking to the residents, three young women who were attending the local university, when one of them asked if we'd heard that frightening screaming and yelling that came from somewhere in the apartments on Saturday night. "We thought that somebody was going crazy, that there was a maniac loose. We nearly called the police." Carol, her face red with embarrassment, explained to them the source of outbursts. The girls laughed and told us not to worry. But I kept the windows closed and my voice down after that, even during the warm late April evenings when the Maple Leafs were competing for the Stanley Cup.

Twenty-five years later, when we lived in a house in Edmonton, Alberta, there was another very warm night and another important hockey game. This time the warm night was in May—the 15th of May 1990 to be exact—and the game was the first in the best-of seven series for the Stanley Cup, the Edmonton Oilers against the Boston Bruins. The game was well into the third overtime period when Petr Klima scored for the Oilers. The sliding doors from the family room to the patio had been open all during the game. Carol, Clare, Andrew, and I shrieked loud and long; our dog Kate started howling; and her wailing woke up the neighbors' dog, who often slept outside.

The next day, the very sweet but a little nosey little old lady who lived in the house behind us said hello to me over the back fence. "I hope everything is alright with your family," she said. "In the middle of the night, I was awakened by an awful noise coming from your place. I didn't know if I should call the police." I assured her everything had been fine and explained about the excitement of the hockey game. "I hope there aren't any more overtime games," she said and, wishing me a pleasant good morning, went inside.

Tonight is the opening game of the 2024 Stanley Cup playoffs and, for the first time since 2006, the Edmonton Oilers are in it, this time against the Florida Panthers, a Miami team that didn't even exist when Petr Klíma had scored his goal and caused the old lady and the dogs of our neighborhood to wake up. It's also the first hockey game I'll have watched at the Little Cabin in the Big Woods at any time, let alone June. I no longer live in Edmonton, but I'm excited that the Oilers are finally in finals, and I'm prepared to offer all the vocal encouragement I can. I'm sure Katrina and Hankie will join in.

That's why, earlier this afternoon, I paid a visit to my neighbor Jeff, who lives three cabins away. Noise travels easily in the quiet nights in the forest, and I was afraid that, if he didn't know about my ways of expressing my enthusiasms, he might become as alarmed as the three young college students had been six decades ago or my aging neighbor in 1990. And, if the game went into three overtimes, the Oilers won, and my joy was excessively loud, I certainly didn't want him to call the local sheriff's office.

Children of the Pioneers

The sons and daughters of the pioneers who built the first cabins at Crooked Lake in the mid-1950s are now in their late sixties and early seventies. In mellow moments, they reminisce about their early summers in the Upper Peninsula. If they lived in the Lower Peninsula, they had, in their infancy, to take a ferry across the Mackinac Straits and travel gravel roads for the last thirty or so miles. There was electricity, but most residents had to pump water by hand and make late night trips to the little building behind their cabins. Radio reception was iffy and television was virtually unheard of. Life was primitive by today's country living standards. But it was nowhere as primitive as the life my mother and her sisters experienced going to the Shawnigan Lake cabin over a century ago.

My father recreated the experience in one of his columns:

As I heard the story, when Pat was a little girl, the family—father, mother, children, dog and cat—boarded the train on the first or second day of the school summer holiday and travelled to Shawnigan to stay there until Labor Day. All but Pat's dad, that is. He commuted on a special train that left the lake Sunday night to take wage-earners to Victoria for their working week and brought them back late Saturday afternoon in time for dinner.

The family left the train at Cliffside station and struggled down the trail with bags, boxes, baggage, and sundry supplies. When they reached the cottage, all their good school clothes were stowed away, a box for each child, and they donned newly bought summer dresses or dungarees and cotton sweaters, received their new running shoes and new bathing suits, and were there for the vacation. If one of them dangled his or her feet over the bow of the rowboat in deep water and dropped a shoe off—as Pat, who had a penchant for such things, did— that was too bad. But small feet grew tough anyhow, even when wild berry picking, and stubbed toes and small thorns were part of the routine.

Each had specific chores. There was water to be carried in buckets, wood to collect, stones to pack for a wall, dirt to sift for a flowerbed above the shore gravel, and for the older girls, household duties as well as small sisters to mind. The days were full, swimming, hiking, berry picking, exploring, rowing a boat, making lemonade, maybe fishing to supplement the groceries their dad brought in with him each weekend, and trips to the little store or nearby farm for milk.

When darkness fell, there were stories to be told, tales of ghosts and goblins so graphic to young minds that an elder had to walk small children of neighbors home through the woods to protect them from the spirits. Coal lamps were lit and carried to the cottage verandah, where small ones were put to bed early.

Sun-baked afternoons echoed with the shouts of children at play, swimming and more swimming, bee stings, mosquito bites, the games of small ones with big imaginations, staple food, the metallic monotone of cicadas, the chattering of squirrels, and scolding jays. You needed a well for cold water when the lake grew warm and also to provide storage for perishables. You gathered scented leaves, tied them with string and hung them hopefully from the privy roof. It was a simple life, a healthy life – and once you were at Shawnigan you were there for the season.

Victoria Daily Times, May 24, 1963

Late Spring Flowers

Walking down to the lake this morning, just over three days before the longest day of the year, I noticed that the pink lady slipper that had been a symbolic promise of the coming blossoms of late spring and the summer to follow had shriveled and turned a dull brown. But along the bank, almost hidden by the green spikes around it, was the first iris flower of the year.

It was a royal blue and rich yellow, much smaller than its domestic cousins. But the reappearance of this hardy survivor each year is, like the appearance of the lady slipper, an announcement of seasonal change. The name is from the Greek word for rainbow, a reference to the fact that the flowers of the various varieties have a range of colors. For us the name is a promise of the variety of flowers of many colors that will appear over the next few weeks around the Little Cabin in the Big Woods.

Already, delicate pink wild roses dot the bank. There used to be many more before passersby decided that the bushes would look good in their suburban gardens, not knowing that the plants usually do not survive the transfer. In my memories, they bloom in profusion. There used to be a clump of them along my morning bike route, and, an hour or so after my ride, a bud from one of the bushes would burst open in the brandy snifter on our window-side table.

In the cleared area around the cabin, there are more recent arrivals, two cheery yellow blossoms: the swamp buttercup and the Canada hawkweed. Both are pollinators and so their yellow flowers do more than just cheer us up on gray days. If there are enough around, it's okay to pick a buttercup and hold it under your chin to see if there is a reflection that says you like butter. If you're Canadian, you realize that you're not the only species in the area from the land of long winters and exciting ice hockey.

At the edge of the cleared area, there are other Canadians. The Canadian anemone, a flower with five white petals and yellow center, was sought by Native Americans for its many medicinal uses. The Canadian bunchberry, which has four white petals that often have rusty markings on the tips, looks like a dogwood. And it is—one of the smallest members of the species that includes the tree that bears the official flower of my home province of British Columbia. Both the anemone and the bunchberry are important pollinators. It is so wonderful to have so many fellow Canadians as company next to the cabin. They brighten the late June days and they contribute to the environment.

Its head rising above the bracken surrounding it, the bull thistle is the last of the recently-blossomed plants. A deep purple, it is a contrast to the shorter yellow and white blooms near it. While it is often considered an invasive species, it does make important contributions to the living beings around it, nectar for pollinators and seeds and nest-lining down for gold finches.

Right next to the side door, I'm greeted by old friends who live there: the forget-me-nots than I raked carefully around when I arrived a month ago. The last of the little flowers of early spring, they will be with me nearly all the summer. Each time I walk up the path and spot the newly-arrived flowers of the changing seasons, I stop in front of them and they evoke for me thoughts about flowers than will never fade: the memories of changing seasons.

Pictures on the Fridge

Like most fridges, ours is decorated with photos, drawings, illustrated magnets, and colorful magnetic clips. Some of the items go back over three decades. That's because, whenever an old fridge loses its cool, we select our favorite "decorations" and transfer them to the replacement.

Among the items covering the front and one side of our current fridge are two magnets for a defunct kennel, another (rather large) one on which is written a long-ago grocery list and a magnetic magic marker. The marker doesn't work anymore, and the grocery list has permanently bonded to the supposedly erasable white surface. There are photos of Andrew and Clare when they were in their thirties, along with three of dearly-departed dogs who were our lakeside companions. Then there are three sketches Clare made many years ago: one of the cabin as seen from the dock, another of a huge bottle of wine (possibly Gallo Red), and a third of a can of Budweiser. We're craft beer aficionados now, but we keep the picture because of Clare's really good artistry.

There is one item that is special beyond all others. It's a photocopy of a 1929 picture of my father and my godfather, my dad's best friend, Jimmy Nesbitt. They are sitting in the newsroom of the *Victoria Daily Times*. My father, not yet twenty, had been hired as a summer replacement at the paper, which Jimmy had joined a year earlier. Jimmy is lounging on the top of his desk, in front of a huge manual typewriter; my father is leaning back in his chair, his feet up on the middle shelf of a bookcase, thoughtfully sucking on a pipe.

What was supposed to be a three-month job for my father turned into a forty-four-year career. He started as a glorified office boy, became a reporter covering sports, city hall, the local courts, and the provincial legislature, was named as associate editor and, in 1950, started writing a column, which appeared several times a week and covered local events and politics, along with lighthearted stories about his being a befuddled husband and father and an incompleat angler (he was actually pretty good). His final column appeared on June 30, 1973, the day of his retirement.

Except for the occasional letter to me, he never wrote another word, but he enjoyed spending time on the waters in front of our Victoria home and at Shawnigan Lake, the places he so loved and had so often written about in his columns.

A quarter-of-a century after his retirement and a few years after his death, I began going through microfilms at the public and university libraries in Victoria, collecting those of his columns that I thought would interest my sisters, along with my children and theirs. I was hearing his voice and learning his style. When I began writing personal essays about Crooked Lake, I would ask myself, "How would my father have done this?" He was becoming my mentor, and I dropped my boring academic style and began following his lead. Now when I look over what I've read, I find that in the things that interest me and in the ways I write about them, I am becoming my father.

As I'm writing this, the photocopy of the old picture is on the desk beside me. I see a couple of things that had escaped my notice before. On his old desk, there is a bunch of newspapers, haphazardly stacked. It looks like a good sneeze would send them to the floor. On the floor there are several crumpled pieces of paper that had missed the waste basket. They probably contained false starts of news stories he was working on.

Then I look around me. On the coffee table, there are files of early drafts of essays, reporters' notebooks, a novel opened to chapter two, and a phone book. But I can't find the phone that is supposed to be there. Under my desk, spilling out from a large cardboard box, are copies of the local Marquette newspaper. I use them to start the morning fire. But when one lands on the floor, it stays there.

I guess I've become my father in more ways than one.

Old News

Today, as part of the annual (sort of) cleaning of the cupboards, I tackled the one that contains the pots and pans. I took everything off the shelves, which I then cleaned with Lysol; I washed the various vessels and re-shelved them in an order only slightly neater than had existed before.

There were a few surprises. On the top shelf, behind a pot lid with a cork for a lifter, there was an old percolator coffee pot of unknown origin that had no lid. On the middle shelf were six haphazardly stacked frying pans of various sizes along with two torn spatter screens to cover all but the largest one. Lying on its side was a bottle of party supplies of a kind that I'd never heard of. It was probably so old that it had been distilled before the term "best before" had been invented.

But the biggest surprise was on the bottom shelf, which was really the kitchen floor covered with a piece of linoleum. I discovered the surprise under the linoleum, which I had lifted out (for the first time) to clean. It was an old newspaper, a *Detroit Free Press* from 1971.The lead stories about the Vietnam War and the divided city of Berlin were interesting. More interesting was a readers' poll in which 51.7 percent of the respondents thought that Spiro Agnew should be kept as Nixon's running mate in 1972. (In 1973, he would be forced to resign in disgrace.)

Most interesting to me was the date of the newspaper: September 4, 1971, the Saturday of the Labor Day weekend. The date evoked wonderful memories. That was the first Labor Day weekend we had spent in the Upper Peninsula. After our June wet-but-happy trip to Colwell Lake in a rented camper, we'd bought our own camper. While people we didn't know were living in a cabin on Crooked Lake, which we hadn't yet heard of, we were parked at Lot 15 at Colwell, where we swam, fished (unsuccessfully), hiked around the lake, and, in the evening, made and ate s'mores while dodging constantly wandering campfire smoke. Andrew, then three-and-a -half, and Clare, one-and-a-half, managed to get most of the gooey treat on their t-shirts.

We discovered Crooked Lake two years later, when a north wind made beach-sitting impossible and we decided to take a hike along a couple of back roads. In 1985, on another hike along the same roads, we discovered that the cabin at Lot 18 Crooked Lake was for sale and, within a month, it was ours and had become the Little Cabin in the Big Woods.

I hope that those 1971 owners of the cabin at Lot 18 loved the place as much as we do. They certainly did a good job of keeping the cupboards neat and clean and left us the coffee pot and two of the fry pans, along a memory-evoking copy of the *Detroit Free Press*. I've tossed the lidless coffee pot and the linoleum, which was too brittle and dirty to put back. But I've kept the newspaper, not as a liner, but as something I'm going to read again this Labor Day. I'm sure that I will experience the melancholy sweetness of remembering a joyous weekend of over half a century ago.

Kingston Plains — The Graveyard of Trees

Along Alger County Road 58 between Munising and Grand Marais, there are plenty of interesting places to stop: vistas overlooking Lake Superior, a beach littered with the remains of ships wrecked long-ago, an historic lighthouse, and a giant sand dune hill that used to be a chute for sliding logs into the lake. There are a lot of interpretive signs at each stop. Of course, you'll have to pay a fee (the minimum is twenty-five dollars per car for a seven-day pass), it may be hard to find a parking spot, and you'll have lots of company.

But just off the highway, there's a very interesting, I think awesome, place that's full of history, has few if any visitors, no interpretive signs and no fees. It's called the Kingston Plains (after a Canadian logging company). Turn onto the Adams Trail

Fig 3-3: **The stumps on the Kingston Plains are ghostly reminders of the clear-cut logging decades of the late nineteenth century**

(it's about twenty-six miles from Munising and begins right where there's a huge parking lot (that's filled with pickup trucks and snowmobile trailers in the winter) and drive about a mile-and-a-half along the gravel road.

To your left you'll see a number of very large (maybe 500 feet across) saucer like- depressions and acres of stumps. You've reached what Clare's partner called the Graveyard of Trees. The saucers are what the geologists term "kettles," created when the glaciers withdrew after the last ice age. Huge blocks of ice would be left behind and over years become covered with debris. When the ice finally melted, the kettles were formed.

The stumps were "created" in the later decades of the nineteenth century by an army of loggers that had moved through, clear-cutting the area before heading further west. Fires that swept through the region in the years that followed cooked the ground so that there was no second growth. The blackened sides of many stumps still bear testimony to those conflagrations.

Yesterday, I visited the Kingston Plains, something I try to do every couple of years. It is a kind of ritual pilgrimage. Occasionally I take friends, and Clare joins me when she's here. But usually I come on my own. There is virtually no traffic and certainly no other people. I can be alone with nature and history. There was something new this time: before I reached the kettles' area, I passed signs that weren't there two years ago. They advertised dog sled rides in the winter, helicopter tours in the summer, and a place to stay called "Naughty Pines." I guess that place offers a chance for something to do after the ride or tour. Not interested: I've got better things to do with my money.

I pulled the car over beside a very large kettle with at least two dozen stumps dotting the spongy ground that covered it. Stepping over the recently-blossomed yellow wood sorrel and ox-eyed daisies that bordered the road, I walked down into kettle. In the distance came the sounds of birds, perhaps robins, from a large serviceberry bush. No doubt their ancestors had visited the place for centuries and, like the traditional Native people, had feasted on the berries. The birds in the trees, along with a grouse wandering on the far edge of the embankment and a black fly that seemed determined to disrupt the serenity I was experiencing were the only other creatures around.

The stumps were of varying heights, depending on the depth of the snow when the trees had been felled. You could see the marks of the undercuts and backcuts made by loggers' axes and misery whips (crosscut saws). The sides of several still bore blackness from the fires. I sat down on the spongy ground beside one of them and looked and listened. The car was less than a hundred yards away, but I was alone in times past where the only sounds of the present came from the robins.

I had been sitting there for half-an-hour when I heard the rumble of not-too-distant thunder and looked up to see dark clouds advancing from the west. I was back in the present. I stood and walked quickly back to the road. Just before the border of flowers, there was an amazing sight: a large stump with an open space at its base out of which grew a small serviceberry bush, a few ripening berries on its branches. In the graveyard of trees, created over a century ago by men, the enduring power of nature was engendering new life.

DIRECTIONS: From the intersection of M 28 and M 94 at Shingleton, take Alger County Road 15 north for four miles; turn right at the Bear Trap Restaurant and proceed 16 miles east on Alger County Road 58 to Adams Trail. Head east a couple of miles along the Adams Trail, noticing the kettles and stumps to the left.

Determined to Know Berries

On my way home from town the other day, I turned onto the two-track that leads to the secret berry patch where, over many decades, I have spent countless contented hours gathering blueberries, the little fruits that are delicious and good for both the body and soul. It was nearly a month until the beginning of miini-giizis, the moon of blueberries, and there would not be much to see, perhaps a few remaining bell-like flowers and some tiny pink fruits that still had the five pointed crowns of the blooms. It would be good to briefly visit this special place and anticipate the coming joys of picking and later sharing blueberry muffins and pies with family and friends.

As I turned back onto the highway, a phrase from Thoreau's *Walden* popped into my head. The nineteenth-century New England writer had written a chapter on a bean field he had planted. In the chapter he had proclaimed that he was "determined to know beans." His learning experience included excursions into ancient history and philosophy, along with social satire and some rather unconventional horticultural tips. I decided that, until the blueberries ripened, I would "know blueberries," a little about them botanically and about the beliefs of the Anishinaabe people for whom these were sacred plants.

I learned that the miini, as the Anishinaabe called them, or, in the language of the botanists, the *vaccinium augustifolium*, are indigenous shrubs whose origins date back over ten thousand years to the end of the last ice age. They are most often found in the sandy soils called pine barrens and grow across the New England and Upper Midwest states, as well as in parts of Ontario, Quebec, and the Maritime provinces. Star-shaped flowers and a sky blue color symbolically link them to the worlds above; rhizomes in the earth create a community by linking the bushes to each other. Hardy plants, they survive brutal winters, returning each year to give their fruits to people and other creatures.

To the Anishinaabe, interrelationships were an essential aspect of the miini. The star crowns on the bell-shaped flowers represented the star people who, at a time of famine and illness among the human people, sent the gift of blueberries to nourish and heal them. The plants were sacred and the first picking was accompanied with joyous ceremonies of thanksgiving in which the celebrants often wore regalia stained with dyes made from the juices of the berries. Picking was also a communal event, with women and children gathering and, while many of the youngsters may have acquired blue stained but washable faces during the activities, they were learning about their relationship to spirit beings and the land and helping their own extended families gather fruits that would provide nourishment and health during the long, cold winters when the plants themselves were surviving in the earth under the snows.

Native peoples shared the gifts of the star people with the newly-arrived settlers from across the sea. It has been suggested that it was not turkey, but sautauthig, a pudding-like dish made from powdered dry blueberries and corn and mixed with water, that they brought to the feast now called Thanksgiving.

Getting to know blueberries was an enriching experience. When miini-giizis, the blueberry moon, arrives and I return to the two-track, it won't just be a matter of enjoying a couple of quiet hours gathering these fruits. I will think about how the shrubs and the gifts they bear are symbols of survival and of community and about the health and joy they bring.

A Missed Ritual

Fig. 3-4: Glorious sunsets mark the end of the long evenings of late spring

Over the years, one of our favorite June rituals has been celebrating the summer solstice. We'd head down to the dock late in the evening and watch the sun sink slowly toward the space between the two very tall white pines at the north end of the lake. As the disk slipped below the horizon, we'd raise our glasses in a toast to the longest day of the year. After the twilight had faded and the first stars appeared in the darkening sky, we'd head back to the house.

One year, when I owned a camera which had a lens that made distant objects seem about two percent closer, I used up a roll of film recording the sun's descent. When I got the prints back, the sun looked like a tiny pinprick, much smaller than it had appeared to the naked eye.

This year, June 20th, the day of the solstice, promised to be sunny and dry, with just enough of a breeze from the south to keep the mosquitoes at bay. But I wasn't on the dock to watch the sun set at the north end of the lake. When that occurred, I was in an airplane flying toward Chicago on the first leg of a journey to the City of the Pavements Gray. There I was picked up by Clare, and, a couple of days later, we began the drive to the Little Cabin in the Big Woods. It was a long journey, often tiring, and occasionally stressful; but it was one we both enjoyed. It was Clare's first trip to the Upper Peninsula in seven years: the care-giving of Alberto after his massive stroke had taken up much of her time and certainly most of her energy. The gentle qualities of the natural world at Crooked Lake, for which she felt the emotion of *querencia* as much as I did, would bring her the healing and rest she so needed.

Just after noon on June 25, our fourth day on the road, we turned off Michigan Highway 94 and began the last part of our journey, the two-mile drive down the road that would become almost a two track by the time we reached the driveway to the Little Cabin in the Big Woods.

"Are you excited?" I asked her.

"Yes," she replied quietly, almost breathlessly.

We didn't talk to each other as we turned into the driveway. I glanced at her. Joy radiated from her face.

It was a hot day, even a little muggy, but cloudless. That evening we walked down to the dock and sat watching the setting sun. The day was fifty-six seconds shorter than it had been on the day of the solstice; but, for reasons I don't understand, the sun set nearly a minute later. We gazed quietly. Clare, who had a good camera, took some wonderful photographs of the minute.

Other people had been enjoying summer for several days. For Clare and me, it began as we sat there together. She would be here for nearly four weeks, and we would cherish every minute.

4   July – Blueberry Moon

July begins with a population explosion. Watercraft cover the surface of the lake: kayaks, rowboats, speedboats, jet skis, pontoon boats. Children's happy shrieks echo along the shore. The smoke of evening campfires drifts through the trees. The laughter of happy vacationers grows louder as the sunlight fades. Lovers of quietness take woodland walks or paddle canoes in the early morning. Blueberry pickers eagerly await the ripening of the harvest, inspecting their secret berry patches every few days.

Fig. 4-1: Watercraft cover the surface of the lake

Can—Oo Canoe?

In the quiet of early morning, I slip the canoe into the lake. The surface is flat except where water spiders swim across it, where my paddle ruffles the surface, and where the stern of the canoe leaves its wake. The pontoon boats, canoes, paddle boats, kayaks and jet skis that will become active as the day warms are tied up to docks or pulled up on shore. Except for a blue kayak that disappears behind a point at the far end of the lake and a turtle, I am alone on the water.

As I paddle and then glide, my mind wanders back to other places and earlier times when I've been on the water in canoes. My father, who had repaired an old canoe and then used it to fish at Shawnigan Lake, gave me my first lessons on paddling and etiquette. "You don't push off from a dock or the shore with the blade of the paddle; if you do that too often, the wood will split or break. Use the butt end. If you hit the side of the boat when you're dipping the blade into the water, you've got the wrong angle and you will slow down." He taught me the j-stroke, where you draw the paddle backward at the end of the stroke, keeping the craft from lurching from side to side. "It's more efficient, and you don't have to keep switching the paddle from side to side. But when you do, and there's someone in the boat in front of you, pass the paddle from one hand to the other behind your back so you don't drip water on your partner."

I remembered these lessons the first time I'd brought Carol to Shawnigan Lake to meet my parents. It was a moonlit night and a canoe trip seemed like a romantic thing to do. As we paddled down the silvery path laid on the water's surface by the full moon, I thought that my romantic hopes would be increased if I enriched the excursion with a moonlight serenade. She endured my renditions of "Cruising Down the River," "Cry Me a River," "Love Me Tender," and a few other of what I thought were mood-enhancing tunes, but when I began Pat Boone's "Friendly Persuasion," she said, "Enough," in a firm but good-natured tone.

In spite of my vocalizations, she accepted my proposal of marriage. However, for years, she would quietly leave the room when I watched "Sing Along with Mitch" on the TV and joined in.

When we acquired the Little Cabin in the Big Woods, we bought a rowboat. It wasn't big, but it seemed bulky and was difficult to head in a straight direction when you could see where you had been but not where you wanted to go. We didn't have a dock yet, and so it was a bear to haul out of the water.

After two years, we traded it in for a canoe, an Old Town 14.5 (as in feet) model. It was made of molded plastic, was forest green in color, and weighed less than seventy pounds. It looked pretty, was easy to carry to the shed for winter storage, and moved across the water like a charm.

Before Carol and I took it out on its maiden voyage, I gave her a crash course version of my father's teachings about canoes. She caught on right away and soon was a better paddler than her teacher. In fact, she would occasionally remind me to push away from the shore with butt end of the paddle and scold me for knocking the side of the canoe. Before each trip, she would sternly command: "Don't sing." We spent many joyous early morning and late evening paddles, all of them without songs, during the few years we shared at the Little Cabin in the Big Woods.

Today, as I reach the north end of the lake, turn model 14.5 around and begin the trip back to the dock, I begin to sing quietly the words of the Frank Sinatra tune, "I'll Be Seeing You in All the Old Familiar Places." My eyes mist up and the lake becomes a blurry vision replaced by the wonderful images of the canoe trips of many years ago.

The Story of a Kayak

On warm, sunny days they dot the surface of the lake; at night they line the shores. They're brightly-colored kayaks. If you listen to the sounds of the paddlers, you can tell that they're a source of great delight. And they have no motors. All that is great; I'm glad that they vastly outnumber the jet skis. They'll all made of molded plastic, they're easy to pull up onto shore and to strap onto the top of a car, and they give their owners opportunities to explore many watery places they might otherwise not encounter.

But they all have a drawback: except for their colors they're all pretty much the same. They're fun to paddle, but they're not really much to look at, and, I'm sure, they have no stories.

That's not the case with one kayak we saw the other day when we were sitting on the dock. It was long, lean, and sleek; its sides were made of strips of different types of wood; and it glided through the waters the way you'd imagine that the craft of the Eskimos of Alaska and Arctic Canada did. We found out that the kayak had a wonderful story.

It belonged to Missy, a neighbor whose father grew up on Crooked Lake and who, herself, had spent over half-a-century of summer vacations here. "I don't remember not having known the lake," she once told us. Boats have always been a part of her summers here. "My Dad used to take me fishing in a little John Boat [a small one with a flat front]." Later she graduated to canoes. Her watercraft often became her reading room. She'd paddle to a quiet corner of Crooked Lake, ship her paddle, and read for an hour or so. Friends and neighbors would keep their boats far away so as not to disturb her.

Several years ago, Missy's father-in-law, who had built boats for himself, said to her: "You have given me the gift of wonderful grandchildren. I'd like to give you a gift. I'd like to make you a boat." Missy and her husband Brian ordered a kit from Chesapeake Bay Lite and the building of a kayak began. But her father-in-law passed away and, because of family tensions and quarrels, Missy and Brain lost track of the half-built kayak. "I thought we'd never see it again," she remembered. "But a couple of years later, one of the relatives called and said the kayak was in their basement. If we wanted it, would we come and take it away."

They did. But they didn't know how to finish constructing it. And then, they had a great piece of luck. While out driving one afternoon, they saw a man working on a canoe in his driveway. "Brian and I stopped and talked to him and asked for his help." Could he finish the kayak for them? He could and would only ask that Brian, an auto mechanic at the time, help him with badly needed repairs on one of his vehicles. "His name was Pat, and he was a boat lover, just like Brian's dad, my dad, and me."

One day, as Missy was watching the building, she noticed something amazing. "When we got home, I asked Brian if he'd noticed Pat's hands. They were just like his father's. It was as if his father's spirit were there to help finish the building he'd started. It made the canoe even more special to us."

They brought the completed craft to Crooked Lake and launched it, with joy and champagne toasts, on October 17, 2017. Pat had accompanied them along with his canoe, and they spent an autumn weekend boating in front of their cabin and showing Pat around to the other little lakes. Missy continues to paddle it joyously every summer.

When I saw the canoe, I was reminded of a line from Shakespeare's "Romeo and Juliet," in which the hero describes his newly-discovered love: "So shows a dove, trouping among crows as yonder lady to her fellows shows." That is what this canoe looked like compared to the plastic ones.

The little molded plastic jobs are fine, but they don't symbolize so many wonderful things. Missy likes paddling and finding a reading spot, but most important to her is the love embodied in the beautiful, sleek craft. "It started with the love of my father-in-law and continued with the loving care Pat put into finishing it. He's become a very good friend. That's all in the canoe."

I don't know the cost of the kayak kit Missy and Brian bought. But you couldn't put a price on the finished product and the love and joy it creates.

Bird-Time and Boat-Time

We have plenty of clocks around our place: the one on the microwave, a really attractive battery-operated wall clock (a gift from

Fig. 4-2: The early-morning squawks of the Sandhill Cranes, the largest of the snowbirds around the lake, signal it's time to get to work

friends who borrowed our place over three decades ago), the one on the bottom of the computer screen, a smart watch (Clare's, not mine), an ordinary watch that just reads out the hours and minutes (mine), and a really old windup clock with hands that glow in the dark. I really have no excuses for being late for an appointment in town or a dinner invite (although I usually am) or for overcooking something in the oven (a frequent occurrence).

But if the power went out, the wall clock ran out of batteries, the smart watch turned stupid, the ordinary watch fell into the water while I was canoeing, or the springs in the windup finally gave out, I wouldn't worry. That's because here at Crooked Lake we have bird-time and boat- time. Bird time is calculated by which avian friends you hear; boat-time by what kind and how many watercraft are on the lake. These times aren't as precise as clock-time, but as accurate as we need out here in the Upper Peninsula's north woods.

If you wake up when it's still dark and a myriad of bird songs reaches your ears (one time, Clare, who was sleeping on the screen porch, logged nearly two dozen on her Merlin Bird ID app), it's probably an hour before sunrise. But if you hear a squawk coming from beyond the tree line and it sounds like a loon with laryngitis, it means that the sand hill cranes are on their way to work. A whirring noise like a small fan coming from just outside the screen porch lets you know the hummingbird has begun his day-long activity of sipping sugar water from the feeder and is driving interlopers away. It's time for you to be up and at it.

After breakfast, when you're gazing out the window finishing your last cup of coffee or outside leaning on your rake, you can tell the time by looking at the lake. If there are no boats or only one or two, perhaps a canoe and a small rowboat, each moving slowly across the water, with the rower or paddler casting a fishing rod, the morning is still early. The boats' occupants are enjoying the quiet that will disappear well before lunch.

When the kayaks come out, it's around eleven. It's vacation time and their paddlers, who are operating on vacation time, have recently awakened. The little boats make no noise, but the vacationers' laughter, happy calls to each other, and their splashing each other with their paddles send the fish scurrying (or whatever fish do when they're alarmed) and the fishermen back to the shore.

There's a quietness as the sun reaches its zenith—it's lunchtime. But soon, it's mid-afternoon. The maritime population swells and the noise level rises. The joyful noise of the kayakers is augmented by the roars of power boats pulling skiers and tubers behind them and sometimes, the roar (or is it snarl?) of jet skis.

The arrival of early evening is signaled by the appearance of a flotilla of pontoon boats that move quietly across the water following the shoreline. The occupants are frequently older people out for a post-prandial cruise. As they pass your dock, their quiet conversations float across the water. They wave to you and you realize that, late diner that you always are, it's past time to leave the dock and start supper.

Dinner over and the dishes washed and put away, you walk to the dock to watch the setting sun. There are no boats on the water and it's so quiet you can hear the loons conversing at the end of the lake. There is no noise from the hummingbird feeder. My co-tennant has finished his all-day sipping.

When the weird calls of a barred owl drift through the darkness, it's time to call it a day. There are no night owls in this cabin.

Scat!

A hundred or so yards from our driveway, where Crooked Lake Drive turns into a barely passable two-track that wanders through the forest, there is a small clearing. On their early morning and late afternoon walks, Hankie and Katrina spend several minutes sniffing vigorously when they reach it, leave what my grandmother used to call their "calling cards," and then proceed with their walks. As a friend of mine says, they're reading and replying to their P-mail.

But this morning, it was different. At the edge of the two-track, there was a pile of black feces that hadn't been there yesterday afternoon. It was the size of the leavings of a large dog and had bits of unidentifiable undigested stuff in it. The dogs sniffed longer and more intensely and left much more detailed responses on it.

Back home, a Google search revealed that what Katrina and Hankie probably already knew: the scat they'd investigated was most likely from a wolf or coyote. Occasionally we hear the coyotes at night, but I've never seen or heard a wolf around here. Some neighbors have, and a few have spoken of seeing wolf paw prints in the summer dust or winter snow. Both species leave their poop at the edge of trails to mark their territories.

It started me thinking. During early July, especially in the days preceding and following the Fourth, there is always a huge influx of human beings into their territory. During the days, ATVs and side-by-sides roar along the two-tracks that lace the forest. At night, the animals have no doubt been terrified by the rockets' red glare and the bombs bursting in air as much as Hankie and Katrina have been. But fortunately, the wolves and/or coyotes don't scratch at the door and climb shivering onto my lap. They retreat deeper into the woods, away from the boundaries of their territories.

It is much quieter now. Many of the cabins are empty, motor traffic through the woods has diminished, and the supply of fireworks has been exhausted. Our wild four-legged neighbors have probably come back to reclaim their territory and have left a message to let us know. It's a message I'll observe and I'll make sure Hankie and Katrina do as well. We have our territory and they have theirs. We'll keep to our side of Crooked Lake Drive, and we won't wander into the woods beyond it.

Of course, if they extend their territory and leave a boundary marker at the end of our driveway, I'll say "Scat! Wait until the cabins at Crooked Lake are closed for the season and then you're welcome to visit our territory whenever you'd like."

I like to think that this would be one good way of maintaining the balance of nature.

The Incompleat Angler

The other day, our neighbor Rick asked if I ever fished. I told him no, that I liked fish, but not fishing. So yesterday, he brought us some fish he'd caught. They were filleted and ready for the pan. Clare covered them with a seasoned batter she concocted, steamed some asparagus and jasmine rice, and we had a gourmet dinner, washed down with the last half of a bottle of good white wine.

I don't know why I'm not interested in fishing. My father was a good fisherman, casting from the end of the dock or trawling while paddling his canoe at the lake. He also rowed a small boat he'd made a mile out into the Straits of Juan de Fuca. He didn't like eating fish, but he liked catching them and sharing his catch with family and friends. Whenever Carol and I visited the lake, he'd prepare a freshly-caught trout for her breakfast.

Over my long life, my fishing expeditions have been few, far between, and totally forgettable, except for one. It took place in the 1970s during one of our first camping trips to Colwell Lake. A few weeks earlier, I'd taken Andrew, who was five-years-old, to his first major league baseball game. Beginning at four o'clock in the morning, he began waking me up to see if it was time to make the two-hour drive from Kalamazoo to Chicago to watch the Cubs at Wrigley Field. We arrived when the gates opened, an hour-and-a-half before game time, watched batting practice, bought souvenir T-shirts, ate barely warm hot-dogs and slurped watered-down sodas, and settled in to view the game. At the end of the second inning, he looked at me through half-closed eyes and muttered: "I'm tired. Can we go home?"

A few weeks later at Colwell Lake, Andrew, having heard about a fishing trip the kids across the street had made with their father, asked if we could go fishing when we went to the lake. We rented a small aluminum rowboat, bought a fishing license (for me), a couple of inexpensive rods, a package of hooks, and a sour cream carton filled with dirt and a dozen worms, that, we were told, were "Canadian Crawlers."

The next day, before the avian aubades had begun, Andrew was ready to go fishing. I told him we couldn't because other campers were sleeping. Around seven, as we got ready to begin the expedition, I asked if he had to go to the bathroom and he replied negatively.

We set out, rowing to a spot on the lake that the camper next door reported was great for fishing. I skewered a worm on a hook, made a cast, and handed the rod to my son. Almost instantly, the bobber sank beneath the water. "I've got a fish," he exclaimed loudly. I told him to reel it in. Unfortunately, he banged the fish on the side of the boat and knocked it loose. The second cast was more successful. He landed the fish; I bonked it on the head, took it off the hook, placed it in a box lined with ferns, and reached for the tub of Canadian Crawlers so that I could re-bait his hook.

"Dad, I have to go to the bathroom."

"Can you hold it?"

"No, I have to go real bad!"

So I reeled in the lines, rowed back to shore, and Andrew headed up to the outhouse beyond our campsite. A few minutes later, we were back on the water, but the fish had disappeared. We cast our lines unsuccessfully for a while, moved to another spot and had no success.

Then we saw Carol at the shore waving to us—it was time for breakfast.

That evening, we had Andrew's first catch with our dinner. The pieces weren't very big, perhaps silver dollar size, but we had two each. They were delicious. That was probably the most expensive fish dinner we ever had. When you factor in boat rental, fishing license, rods, and Canadian Crawlers, each morsel probably cost more than five dollars.

But the memories remain—and they are priceless.

Let There Be Light — And a Radio

A couple of years ago, the local telephone company installed wonderful new cable modems in all the cabins at Crooked Lake, elevating all of us from the primitive lives we had been leading there. Now we can spend as much time as we want looking at whatever we want on our computer screens. We don't have to waste time looking out the windows at the world of nature to see wonderful things.

A similar event happened when I was fourteen-years-old. The power company had run power lines close to our cabin at Shawnigan Lake. Before, we had been living primitively: we hauled water in buckets from the lake, used a woodstove for cooking and heating water, and at night, lit Coleman lanterns. When my mother announced that she had decided that we'd get electricity into our cabin, my father wrote this humorous column. (Note: Leo Lassen was a gravel-voiced announcer of baseball games that I listened to every night.)

I've been told by the person who makes decisions in our house that we're putting electricity into the shack at Shawnigan this year. I've been told that before and have countered it with the query, "You mean we're buying new batteries for the flashlight?" This time, facetiousness will get me nowhere. I could say, "Look. You put electric light in here and you realize how the cobwebs will show up?"

I could say that, but I know the answer. "Cobwebs, whaddaya-know? You'll just have to use that long-handled broom, won't you?" Sure, I could battle it out, like the dairy interests against colored margarine, and with the same results. So, as my mother taught me, I acquiesce to the inevitable.

Now there are a dozen good reasons for electricity in the shack at Shawnigan. But when electric light comes into the shack, something's going out, and it could be me or serenity, or both. I do most of my vital living up at Shawnigan. There I live dangerously. If you don't believe it, watch me light a Coleman lantern sometime. As far as I know, I'm the only person who has to build a bonfire to light a Coleman—and one hasn't blown up on me yet.

And I do a bit of picturesque brooding by the hearthside glow up at Shawnigan. That's the atmosphere I need to get into the right brooding attitude. Beyond that, I usually get to bed early up there. The light's too bad for reading. With electricity, there's no telling when I'll retire.

But that's not the important part. Without electricity up there, I have no radio—just peace, perfect peace. When we connect up, there'll be heavy pressure for listening to every lacrosse and baseball game on the air. Those are swell games, but I can do without them second-hand. And somehow, I don't cotton to the idea of making Leo Lassen my vocal companion in the calm of a summer's evening.

Beyond that, there'll be a new campaign, once we get electricity, for the benefits of running hot and cold water. You can do it easily with an electric pump—easily, that is, if you can raise a small mortgage. After that will come the fancy bathroom. Who knows the wild ambitions that will be born?

Up to now, there has been a certain sanctuary in Shawnigan, a certain quiet, a restfulness, a freedom from the gadgetry that makes town living so softly irritating. It has been possible to feel that you're away from it all up there. In a pampered sort of way, a man could pretend he was roughing it, showing the frontier spirit, being one with the wilderness.

So now we're going to have electricity. Ah, wilderness—farewell. Goodbye Dan'l Boone, goodbye. And move over squirrels, I'll be up on the branch beside you before September's out.

Victoria Daily Times, January 20, 1954

My Grandfather's Chair

In the living room of the Little Cabin in the Big Woods there are two aging easy chairs. They look out on the lake or, when the weather is really bad, they are turned to face the fire place and (I blush to admit it) the TV set.

Both are what I call "retirement" chairs, and both have histories.

The first is a "reconditioned" lazyboy. I bought it nearly thirty years ago at a store (now long gone) that sold used chairs that had served as trade-ins for new ones. They were spruced up and sent to small towns in the Upper Peninsula, where they were snapped up by summer residents like me and taken to cabins to spend their retirement years. At first, it reclined and I often dozed off. Now the reclining mechanism is nonfunctional, but the chair still rocks gently and I still doze off.

The other is a true retirement chair. A Cogswell easy chair, it was given to my grandfather in July 1938 (a year-and-a-half before I was born) by his fellow workers after he left his job of thirty-two years at the *Victoria Daily Colonist*. It sat in the living room of the basement flat (which looked out on the ocean) to which my grandmother and he had moved when we took over the main floors of the family home. He spent twenty-five years gathering driftwood from the water, listening to the radio, tending the open fire, and sitting in his chair, reading.

After he had passed away, it became my father's chair. In his retirement, he too gazed at the ocean, often fished in his little rowboat, and enjoyed his evenings sitting in the chair reading, tending the fire, and watching westerns on TV. My mother reupholstered it, and, after my father's passing and my retirement, it became mine. It travelled to Edmonton, then to Hartford Connecticut, and then to the Little Cabin in the Big Woods.

As was the case in my grandfather and my father's homes, it looks out on the water and, if you turn sideways, you can see just outside window the woodpile I've made. I often sit in the chair as I sip my morning coffee and make my writing and wood chopping plans for the day. Later I watch the hummingbirds come to the feeder, and if it's windy, the whitecaps racing southward down the lake. On cool evenings, I read as the wood in the fireplace crackles and the rays of the setting sun shine through the trees.

When I sit in it, I think of my grandfather and my father. I have inherited so much from them, not just this retirement chair. They have taught me to appreciate the simple joys of life. And that brings me great happiness.

The First Harvest

It's the end of the first week of *Miini-Giizis*, the blueberry moon. Over the last month, I've been learning about blueberries and making occasional trips to inspect my secret blueberry patch (SBP). There has been some rain, the days have become sunnier, and the nights warmer. It's time to gather my first harvest.

Fig. 4-3: The long-awaited wild blueberry harvest begins, but not before we give thanks for the gift from the spirit beings.

There's a ritual to be followed for my most anticipated event of the summer. I dress in long work socks, a very old pair of corduroys that are thin and shiny at the knees, a green and frayed work shirt, the cruising vest I used to wear when I worked in the woods sixty years ago, and a beekeepers hat with face-covering mesh. It has never occurred to me to wear anything else. I won't until these vestments become unwearable.

From a shelf on the screen porch, I gather a kiddy's sand pail. Carol bought it decades ago at a Manistique sidewalk sale. "It's bright pink," she remarked. "So you won't lose sight of it and accidentally kick it over." Inside it is a square piece of aluminum foil that's wide enough to cover the picked berries in case I do kick the pail over.

I say goodbye to the dogs, who look woebegone. Dogs aren't good blueberry-picking companions. I learned that long ago, when, before I'd acquired the pink pail, a long-gone four-legged friend had knocked over a coffee can and gobbled up its contents. I head to the car and am about to begin the 5.9 mile drive to the SBP, when I realize I've left the pail on the kitchen counter. I go back to the house, explain to Hankie and Trina that I'm not back to stay, retrieve the container and start off again.

I feel a twinge of nervousness as I slow down to turn onto the two-track. Will there be enough blueberries? Will there be another blueberry picker there, or has one been there before me? There are no cars, and, as I drive slowly toward my parking spot, I spot a lot of berries.

"Yes!" I say to myself, as my anxiety dissipates and the joy of beginning the activity I'd been dreaming about all winter in the City of the Pavements Gray surges through me. I park the van off the road, roll down the windows and put my keys and wallet on the dashboard. I don't want them to fall from the pockets of my cruising vest. I tuck the cords into the long gray work socks, put some mosquito lotion on the back of my hands, pull the mesh over my face, grab my pink pail and head to the spot where ripe berries seem most plentiful. I should at least be able to harvest three cups of the tiny sweet fruits, one for muffins we'll enjoy in a few of days, two more for Clare to take back to Albuquerque.

I step over the small bank that separates the road from the field and sit in the middle of a clump of bushes that bear the most fruit. I nestle the pail firmly between two stems, lean forward, and pick the biggest berry on the branch before me. But I don't drop it into the pail. I remember the section in Anishinaabe author Louise Erdrich's *Books and Islands in Ojibway Country* in which she describes the people's first blueberry picking expedition of the season, one in which thanks is given for the gift of these wondrous foods. I am thankful. I think of the goodness of nature and of the joy my first-picking gives me and then pop the berry into my mouth. It tastes sweet and juicy and I'm sure it is good for me, physically and spiritually.

Then I begin to fill the pail to what I estimate is the three-cup level. First I pull a berry-laden branch toward me, put my other hand palm up under the branch and roll my thumb over the fruit so that it falls into my palm. Time moves neither quickly or slowly as I pick. It ceases to exist; the only reality seems to be the rolling of my thumb (which soon turns purple), the feel of the berries dropping into my hand, and the gentle noise as I put them into the pail. When I reach my quota and picking fatigue starts to set in, I cover the pail with the foil, stand up, stretch, and head to the car.

Back at the cabin, I give the dogs a few blueberries to win back their affections and then begin to sort the fruit, discarding berries that are green or mooshed, picking off stems from some, discarding twigs and leaf bits that have made it into the pail, and squishing the occasional bit of living protein that has become mixed with the harvest. I fill three baggies, each with a cup of berries, and put them into the freezer. Then I change out of my cords, which have become damp with the morning dew and have acquired a purple spot on the seat from a bush I'd inadvertently sat on.

I'm a little sore and stiff, and somehow I've acquired a mosquito bite behind my ear. But it's a small inconvenience considering the great joy of spending a morning that I've looked forward to for so long and that I'll remember on those winter mornings when I slide a tray of blueberry muffins into the oven.

A Peaceful Brunch and a Quiet Day

Fig. 4-4: Even on gloomy days, the black-eyed Susans of summer bring sunshine

It's mid-Sunday morning. We sit on the screen porch, enjoying mimosas and nibbling on warm muffins filled with blueberries picked just a few days ago. From the kitchen floats the aroma of a baking Christmas morning wife saver casserole. We sit quietly, sniffing and sipping, looking and listening.

There are no sounds from our next door neighbors, who are no doubt still sleeping. They had celebrated the night until the wee small hours of the morning, engaging in boisterous conversations and raucous laughter and playing cacophonous music that drowned out nature's night sounds—the hoots of barred owls, the ululations of the loon family, the yipping chorus of coyotes. It had not been a silent night.

Like us, our avian neighbors are enjoying brunch. There is a whirr and chirping as our hummingbird approaches the feeder just beyond the screen. Somewhere from the trees behind the Little Cabin in the Big Woods, the tap-tap-tap of a woodpecker faintly echoes. It's not the heavy-metal pounding of its mating call.

There is little activity on the lake. The jet skiers who spent yesterday afternoon churning up the water and roaring back and forth, up and down the one-mile length of the lake, have no doubt run out of gas, both literally and metaphorically, and, are sleeping the morning away. Along the far shore, the gentle purr of a small electric motor seems to follow in the wake of a small canoe, which is piloted by a man in search of a new fishing location. An adult loon and a surviving chick swim their way to the south end of the lake, often disappearing as they dive for their brunch.

The sky, which had been dun for much of the week, is now azure. Occasionally a little, white puffy cloud drifts across it. A slight breeze ripples the lake's surface, and the aspen and birch leaves, now wearing the rich green of midsummer, tremble as the breeze reaches the shore. The white daisies, black-eyed Susans and dandelions in front of the cabin sway back and forth.

A ping from the kitchen demands our attention. The Christmas morning wife saver is ready to be taken from the oven. Christmas is over five months away, but here, at the Little Cabin in the Big Woods, all is calm, all is bright. We finish our muffins and lift our glasses in a toast to the morning.

The rest of the day, Clare is very quiet. Tomorrow, she and two frozen bags of blueberries will head back to New Mexico. Just before sun sets, she goes to the dock to take a final picture of the lake. She posts it on line with the following caption, "In my nearly 40 years of enjoying this place, I have never, ever felt this sad to leave."

Confessions of a Bird-Brain

This morning, as I slipped the canoe into the smooth, calm water and began my (not quite) daily paddle, I noticed the loon chick and its now single parent a couple of hundred yards off to the left. Then suddenly, the chick disappeared beneath the water. Had it been caught by a snapping turtle or a pike? The parent seemed unperturbed, and, several seconds later, the child popped to the surface. I was elated—the time for their departure was getting closer—and at last the chick had learned an essential skill. If it intended to become a successful snowbird in September, it had not only to learn to fly, but also to dive and catch fish.

All was quiet as I continued across the water. Then suddenly a cacophony of warning calls erupted from the end of the lake. A mallard, followed by three ducklings, came out of the sky and landed, too close to the resident birds. The warning calls went on for a few minutes, until the ducks swam up the lake and into the distance.

I was relieved that the loon parent and child had not been hurt. But I was confused and filled with questions. There hadn't been mallards on the lake for well over a decade. What had happened to drive them away? Why had these ones appeared? Were they going to stay or were they just stopping on the way somewhere else? Had their lease at another lake expired, or were they the first snowbirds of the season? After they'd swum to the north end of the lake, I didn't see them again.

I finished my excursion and had begun morning chores when I heard more caterwauling. It was closer to the near shore, louder and sustained. I hurried down to the dock. A bird was swimming toward the loons. I ran back up to the house, grabbed my binoculars and returned to the dock. The bird dove like a loon, but it seemed to be shorter and plumper and floated higher in the water. Perhaps it was a merganser, but I wasn't sure. The chick moved a dozen or so yards behind its mother as the intruder came closer. He and the parent seemed to be having a conference with each other. The youngster kept a polite distance. Maybe it wasn't a merganser but another lone adult loon who was trying to strike up an acquaintance, perhaps inquiring if it might fly south with our loons and then return with them to Crooked Lake next spring to set up housekeeping?

If that was so, the "interview" mustn't have gone to well. In the evening, only our two loons were swimming at this end of the lake. And there was something odd—while the parent dove frequently, the chick had stopped diving. Maybe the chick was male and had decided to protect his mother, keeping unwanted visitors, or maybe suitors, away while she was under water getting her dinner. I just don't know.

Long, long ago, when I'd done something dumb or asked a question my sisters considered foolish or just plain stupid, they would call me a "bird-brain." Today, I wish I had a bird brain; I wouldn't be so confused.

The Woodman Cometh

Usually I order a load of wood every two years. But after a cold and often wet May and June, I've almost run out of the stuff I got last year. The new load arrived yesterday. I'll probably use a bit of it before I leave in a few weeks. The rest will be stacked and next spring will be well-seasoned and ready to warm the cabin.

"You've got trees all around you," a city-bound friend once remarked. "Why don't you cut your own firewood?" I explained that it wasn't that easy. First, the Forest Service prohibits individuals from cutting down living trees for personal use. You are allowed to cut up fallen trees and branches, but if you do, you need to get a permit and there's a limit to what you can cut. But for me, there's a bigger problem. Even if I got a permit, I wouldn't be able to do the job. I'd need a chainsaw, and I don't own a chainsaw and have never used one. At nearly 85-years-old, I'm not going to buy or borrow one and learn how to operate it. If I did, I'd be a menace to standing trees and myself. Should someone take a video of me at work, they might call it "The Incredible Yooper Chainsaw Self-Massacre."

So that's why I buy my firewood. But that too is a difficult process. You need to find someone who sells decent wood. One time, the pieces I got were too bulky to fit into the firebox; another time, they were too long. Then there was the time the guy brought stuff that had been lying on the ground far too long and was well into what Robert Frost called "the slow smokeless burning of decay." Nearly all of it was punk wood. Another time, a fellow brought a load half of which was ironwood. That's a very heavy wood—don't drop a piece on your foot—that burns very slowly and very hot. The slow is ok, but the hot is dangerous for a little stove that's tucked into a corner of the living room. I spent half an afternoon sorting the ironwood from the rest of the load and then creating two racks of wood. Ten years later, the ironwood had slowly decayed, and I put it in the back of the van, drove down a nearly overgrown two track, and deposited the stuff next to a log pile that was also decaying.

Then, three or four years ago, someone recommended Chris, a Yooper who supplements his retirement income by cutting and delivering firewood. At my request, he makes sure that the pieces aren't too big or too long. There is no iron or punk wood, and his price is very reasonable, much less than that of the ironwood or punk wood guys. He arrived today.

I began to stack the wood, most of it outside, and covered it with a tarp, and some in the shed so that it would be good and dry and ready for me next May. I remembered the old saying that firewood warms you three times: when you stack it, when you split it for kindling and starter logs, and when you burn it. It was a warm morning and after a half-hour of stacking, I took off my work shirt. Warming number one.

My shirt was pretty damp and, as I hung it on a hook in the shed, I thought about my grandfather. He had loved fireplaces all his life—there were two in his house. After his retirement, his principal enjoyment was collecting driftwood from the sea just below our home. He'd haul it up to a sawhorse, using a winch for larger heavier pieces, then, using a buck saw, cut it to the lengths he wanted, split it, and stack it in piles. When he finished each afternoon, his shirt and undershirt would be soaking wet and my grandmother would make him change before he was allowed to lay wood in the fireplace, light it, sit in his Cogswell chair, and listen to classical music on the radio.

I got half of my wood stacked yesterday, with time out for a swim and a nap. This morning, the weather forecast called for heavy rain starting at noon. I donned a new work shirt and worked up quite a sweat piling the remaining wood. I finished just as the first drops fell. I hung this shirt next to the one I'd soaked yesterday. Tomorrow, weather-permitting, I'll split a bunch of kindling and starter pieces before I hang up another shirt. That will be the second warming.

The third warming will take place a couple of nights from now. It's scheduled to be much colder and there's more rain forecast. But I'll be warm and cozy inside, watching the flickering flames. I'll probably smile and think about my grandfather. His house had an efficient coal furnace; he didn't need to have a morning and evening fire nearly every day from late September to late April and to spend so many hours gathering driftwood for it. It would be much more efficient for me to install a propane heater. I could drive out the early morning chill and the rainy day dampness by turning a dial. But for my grandfather not working with the wood that that warms three times would have robbed him of a great, but simple pleasure.

And it's the same with me.

Peninsulas

When I was growing up on Vancouver Island, I could look from our lawn across the waters of the Strait of Juan de Fuca to the towering, snowcapped mountains of the Olympic Peninsula. At the University of British Columbia, which was located on Vancouver's Point Grey Peninsula, my dorm window looked out over Howe Sound and the North Shore Mountains.

Just after we moved to Kalamazoo, Michigan in the late 1960s, I was told that the state's motto was *si quaeris peninsulam amoenam, circumspice*: "If you seek a pleasant peninsula, look about you." There were two main peninsulas, the Lower Peninsula, "The Mitten," and the Upper Peninsula, "The Upper Hand." The people living in the former felt smug; those in the latter, superior.

In 1971, when we began to spend extended summers in the Upper Peninsula, we had to drive eight hours to get to the UP. Now, it takes four-and-a half days. Always we've had to cross a bridge, from the Mighty Mac to the little bridge of the Montreal River in the eastern UP. When we reach the Upper Peninsula, we feel that, for a while, we are escaping the life of the city, its hustle and bustle, its problems large and small, its pressing responsibilities. The Upper Peninsula is not cut off from the world we leave behind but is somehow separated from it.

Over the years, we have discovered that the Upper Peninsula we have come to love is the starting point for visits to three famous peninsulas. Off of Highway 2 is the Garden Peninsula, the home of the restored nineteenth-century smelting town, Fayette, and the Stonington Peninsula, on the tip of which, for countless centuries, thousands of monarch butterflies have congregated before beginning their annual fall migration to Mexico. In the north, the rugged Keweenaw Peninsula juts out into Lake Superior. Along the road to its tip, Copper Harbor, are numerous signs announcing the sites (some open to the public) of many of the mines that flourished in the last half of the nineteenth century and into the early twentieth. A trip to any one of these peninsulas is a trip to the past, recent and distant, a sojourn from travelling the highways of the busy modern world.

We've visited these peninsulas often in our many summers spent in the "Upper Hand." When we do, we're not alone. These are favorite tourist spots. But there's another peninsula that's very small, probably a couple of hundred yards long and the same width, that has no name, and hardly anyone visits. It's our favorite peninsula of them all. It's located across our lake, a few hundred yards from the cabin. In the morning we watch the rays of the rising sun shine on it. Late in the summer, the sun sets behind it.

Geologists from Michigan State University have discovered traces of its having been visited by early woodland people thousands of years ago. In the nineteenth century, armies of loggers who left stumps along our shore seem to have missed this little peninsula. The Forest Service has wisely not allowed cabins to be built on it. From our spots on the east side of the lake, we can look across to a place of untouched nature.

This morning, I paddled the canoe to the peninsula. The water was mirror calm, and the loon, its chick, and I were the only ones cutting across it. I landed almost directly across from our place, looked back at the eastern shoreline dotted with docks and pontoon boats, climbed the small bank, and disappeared into the woods. The bracken that covered the forest floor was unbroken. Perhaps I was the first person to walk here this season. There were no trails. The white pines towered high; there were no stumps to stumble into. I sought out spots that provided a view of the lake where there weren't any summer cabins. A squirrel chirred somewhere else on the peninsula.

I felt like the only human being around. And I gave the little peninsula a name, "mewinzha," an Anishinaabe word meaning "long ago." The short canoe trip across the lake had taken me briefly to a different world and to a time when it had been visited by people who lived in harmony with nature.

The Final Harvest

When I drove Clare back to the City of the Pavements Gray, we took two frozen bags of blueberries, two-thirds of the season's first harvest, with us. They were well-packed in ice and, every evening along the way, we'd put them in the tiny freezer at the top of the little motel fridge. The small cooler in which we'd put the berries was the first thing unpacked when we arrived in Albuquerque and the little bags were promptly stored in the freezer.

A day or two later, I unthawed one of the bags and made a batch of muffins, which we took to the nursing home to share with Alberto and his friends. "This is a taste of Michigan's Upper Peninsula," I told them. "These berries were a gift from nature and were still on the bush ten days ago."

Since my return to the Little Cabin in the Big Woods, I've revisited the secret blueberry patch frequently, and the harvest has been bountiful. The three bags of the first harvest had taken two-and-a-half hours to pick. Now I was reaching and exceeding my quota in under an hour. There were lots of clusters of big, plump berries, and when I rolled my thumb over them they would almost cascade into the palm of my hand.

This morning I checked so see how many berry-filled Jiffy bags were in the freezer. A couple more cups of blueberries and I'd have enough to make muffins for our celebratory Sunday brunches—the two equinoxes, Christmas, Clare's and my birthday—as well as a blueberry (not pumpkin) pie for Thanksgiving dinner. I'd have enough left to make a couple of batches for the nursing home at Christmas.

I set out for the secret berry patch and, soon after my arrival, I figured out that this would probably be my last visit for the summer. The secret berry patch was no secret any more. In the four days since my last expedition, several people had been there. Some bushes were picked clean, others had only small berries. And, because there hadn't been much rain, there were a lot of b.b.'s, tiny dry berries that looked like bits of shot, and, because there had been a lot of hot, dry weather, a lot of what we used to call "wrinkle" (as in shriveled) berries. I knew that the birds and, perhaps the bears, would enjoy them and help scatter the seeds.

Nevertheless, I was determined to pick my quota. There were no mosquitoes, and the no-se-ums that had made my forehead look like that of a teenager who had run out of Clearasil had disappeared. But the first horsefly of the season had arrived and was determined to have a part of me for lunch. I placed the pink pail firmly between two stems and sat very still. After a few minutes, he was no longer a threat and I resumed picking.

It took well over two hours to reach my quota. I was beginning to feel dry in the mouth and thirsty. There were faint rumbles of thunder coming from the west. It was time to head to the car. But before stepping from the berry patch onto the two-track, I said a quiet thank you to the spirits who had given the people the gift of *miini*, blueberries. All winter, this gift would not only become part of bountiful brunches and batches of muffins taken to the nursing home, but also the sources of memories that would bring peace and joy to the soul.

Paul Bunyan at Miner's Castle

Fig 4-5: Miner's Castle near the south end of the Pictured Rocks National Lakeshore is both strikingly beautiful but dangerous to those who disobey warnings. (Photo: Danielle Renwick)

Today, I made my first trip to Miner's Castle in a long time. It was glorious as usual, but quite a contrast to my visit, a few weeks earlier, to Kingston Plains. Then I was the only person on the scene, there was no entrance fee, and I was my own interpreter. Now, I was one of several dozen. The occupants of cars from many states had parked, paid the twenty-five dollar a car fee (for a seven-day pass to the entire National Lakeshore), and followed the paved walkways past many interpretive and warning signs.

The first sign, just beyond the visitors' center, indicated the beginning of a 4.5 mile stretch of the North Country Trail from Miner's Castle to Munising and warned that the trail was for foot traffic only and that no pets were permitted. A few yards away, another sign prohibited the flying of drones in the park.

The first major stop was at the Upper Lookout platform. Just beyond the restraining fence, the cliff dropped sharply, perhaps one hundred feet into deep blue water. To the west, the magnificent cliffs of Grand Island rose from the East Channel, while to the north stretched the seemingly immeasurable vastness of Lake Superior, whose steel gray color seemed to merge into an equally gray sky. A few hundred feet away stood Miner's Castle, a stone pillar that gave the area its name. A thousand foot pathway led downhill to a platform only a dozen or so yards from the castle. Through the trees to the north, visitors could see a beautiful sandy beach and, beyond that, the miles of multi-colored cliffs that give the Pictured Rocks their name.

Along the path to the Lower Viewing platform, the signs increased and they weren't interpretive. They were warnings. "Stop: No Travel Beyond This Point," commanded the first, "Violators Will Be Fined and/or Arrested." Smaller ones, every few feet, announced: "Area Closed." And on the railing supposed to stop people from climbing the castle, a big one that, after commanding, "Keep Off Miner's Castle," warned, "It is highly unlikely you will survive a fall." A couple of people in front of me laughed nervously when they read the sign and tightly held the hands of their children. "I can't believe anyone would be so stupid as to try to climb the rocks," the father said.

But some people who were either stupid or couldn't read had. A couple of years ago, a braggart had announced to his friends that he'd climb Miner's Castle. He did, and, when he got to the top, he was too frightened to get down. He had to pay the costs of rescuing him, which were at least three thousand dollars.

The Lower Observation platform provides a good view of the Upper One. There are little rocky outcrops on the way down and at the edge of the water a ledge of somber-looking rocks that slopes into the water. "You'd never survive a fall from there," the mother of the children remarked. Some who have recklessly clambered over the fence and peered over the edge haven't.

As I looked over at the cliffs, I remember a visit I'd made ten years ago. I was writing a story about Paul Bunyan, using as my source an earlier tale about how he had left the earth when he fell over a cliff, landed on a sandy beach, and rebounded, trampoline-like so high that he landed on Venus. "I'll set the story at Miner's Castle," I had thought to myself and went to take a photograph of the area to accompany the tale. But when I got there, there was no beach. If I wanted to use a photograph, I'd have to change the story.

This is how it came out. Paul, who was a bit of a botany hobbyist, had been walking a path by the cliffs when he spotted a flowering plant he'd never seen before and decided to pick it. But he leaned over too far and fell. Nimbly he somersaulted, landing on the sand below, and began rebounding several times. Each time he compacted the sand more and more, turning it into rock. And that's how the ledge that slopes into the water at the base of the cliff was formed.

DIRECTIONS: From the traffic circle in Munising, head 5.4 miles east on Alger County Road 58, then turn north on H-12, and proceed 5.4 miles to the parking lot.

5   August – Fading Summer

The days of early July are filled with activity. As the month progresses, the pace slows. August is a much mellower month. The lake is quieter; several of the summer visitors have returned to their city homes. For many, the highlight of each day is the evening cruise in a pontoon boat. The loon chick is almost as big as its parent; the baby turkeys feeding on the highway right-of-ways are almost full-grown. The leaves have lost their mid-season luster; an occasional branch turns scarlet and gold. A sense of quietness, of an ending, broods over the lake and the land. One is reminded of lines in Robert Frost's "The Ovenbird." "The question that he [the ovenbird] frames in all but words / Is what to make of a diminished thing." My answer: "Embrace and enjoy!"

Calendars

"What's the weather like there?" I get that question quite a lot from friends who live in much warmer and much drier climates. "It can get chilly at night in late May or early June and it rains quite often," I tell them. "But we get a lot of really nice days in the high 70s or low 80s. Once it even got to be 100 degrees. We'd gone to town to see the circus and it was so hot that they had lifted the sides of the big top way up to let breezes from the lake get through."

But now, I have some definite answers and specific numbers to give them. You see, since 2008, I've been writing the daily highs and lows, along with the weather, on a wall calendar that, at the end of the summer, I put in the desk drawer. This year, it was time to tidy the drawer, throwing away old bills, instruction booklets for fridges and microwaves that quit working long ago, and some clippings from the local paper that I once thought were interesting. But I didn't throw away the old calendars and, in fact, spent a rainy day looking over

Fig. 5-1: The fringed gentians of later August are reminders that autumn is not far away

them and making some notes. Now, when people ask about the weather, I'll have facts and figures to bore them with.

Here they are. I usually spend between eight and twelve weeks each summer at the Little Cabin in the Big Woods., arriving in late May or mid-June and leaving around Labor Day. But twice I arrived in the middle of May, and once I left the day after the Autumn Equinox. In 2016, half of the seventy-six days at the lake had temperatures in the 80s. One time that year, it reached 93, and I spent much of the "happy hour" standing up to my neck in the lake, holding above the water a plastic glass filled with gin-and-tonic. At night, it gets below 50 frequently, and, in May and early June, and later September, it dips well into the 30s. In 2011, it reached 30 degrees. It would have been a three-dog night, except I only had one dog with me that year.

It certainly does rain, usually every four or five days. But a couple of times we've had stretches of six days, and then we often looked out the back window to see if the forest animals were walking along the road, two-by-two, seeking a very large boat or at least much higher ground. On the other hand, we've had a few frighteningly long dry spells—a couple of eleven days and another of thirteen. They're often accompanied by hot and brisk winds. If we smell smoke, we become very alarmed. Has an unattended campfire at the campgrounds a mile away gotten out of control? Are the winds bringing news of large conflagrations in the forests a few miles away?

Our yearly weather calendars have interesting photographs of the Upper Peninsula. But every year we also have a calendar with flower pictures. It's not like the ones our old English relatives used to send as Christmas gifts, the ones with pictures of country gardens or fields of golden daffodils. It's a calendar we look at when we gaze out the window or walk along the lakeside path. It's not precise and it doesn't indicate the month or days. But it tells us about the gradual progress of the Upper Peninsula's all-too-short spring and summer.

When the piled snowdrifts under the trees melt away, the serviceberry bushes come into full bloom and then the white petals float to the ground as the winter's last snow falls. By mid-May, the tiny star-flowers, pussy-toes, forget-me-nots, and gay wings poke their heads above the ground. As the days rapidly grow longer, here and there a lone lady slipper announces that the taller, brighter blooms of summer are on the way. Around the solstice, the short-lived blue iris along the lake's bank sway in the warming breeze. By early July, the daisies and the dandelions spring up in the clearings around the cabin. Then, in later August, as the days get shorter, the orange hawkweed and the fringed gentian remind us that autumn will soon arrive and that it will be time to leave.

After the Labor Day weekend, the wall calendar filed away and the car packed, we take the year's final walk down to the lake. Purple asters, goldenrod, and yellow saw thistles sway in the almost chilly breeze. These are the final blossoms on our floral calendar. Next spring we'll have a new wall calendar with different pictures for each month. But our flower calendar will be the same, guiding us through nature's seasons around the Little Cabin in the Big Woods.

Me and the Night Visitors

This morning when I took the dogs out for a walk, I was immediately surrounded by an army of mosquitoes. It was the first time it had happened in a while. Last night had been the warmest in a couple of weeks, and that must have liberated them from the many pools of standing water along the two-track behind the Little Cabin in the Big Woods. I rushed back into the house, put on my mesh-covered hat and sprayed bug-juice on my hands and the ripped knees of my very old jeans. Except for the very loud whining of dozens of the nasty little creatures, the walk went as usual.

That afternoon, bored with a tedious, routine chore I'd been putting off for several days, I decided to turn on the computer and search out mosquito myths of the Native peoples. I couldn't find any from the Anishinaabe of the Upper Peninsula, but I found one from the Oneida people of New York and another from the Tlingit of northern British Columbia.

The former was about a cannibalistic monster that a brave young man killed and burned up. The ashes floating into the air turned into tiny mosquitoes that have been avenging its death ever since. The latter was about two giant mosquitoes who lived at the edge of a river and killed the people passing by in their canoes. The monsters were destroyed by a group of brave warriors, but from their bodies rose hordes of small mosquitoes, also bent on revenge.

I also learned that the loggers of the upper Midwest told stories of Moskitto, a giant mosquito that inhabited the swamps of the north country and that, in warmer weather, would rise from the swamps and fly through the forests looking for people to carry away and blood-let at her leisure. I wondered if she made excursions to Crooked Lake.

I also learned some facts, two of which I found disturbing. It seems the blood-loving insects are attracted to people with O-type blood and that people who drink beer are more likely to get bites than those who don't. I'm O-type and, in order to get accurate information for my books about craft beer, I really do have to engage in "field" research.

Before I went to bed last night, I dabbed some bug-juice around my ears and across my forehead. I didn't want to be awakened by the nasty sound of a mosquito looking for a snack. But, I'd been asleep for a a few hours when I was disturbed by what sounded like the porch door opening. I guess I hadn't pushed it closed properly before retiring. I looked at the clock: it read 2.15 a.m. I was about to drag myself out of bed and shut it tightly when I heard voices and sat up completely awake.

There, silhouetted in the bedroom doorway were two very large mosquitoes. They were whispering back and forth to each other in voices that sounded like Alvin and the Chipmunks, only whinier and louder. They seemed to be arguing.

"Let's eat him now," said one.

"No, let's take him home and eat him later."

They went back and forth for two or three minutes. Then, the "now" voice, whining much louder and sounding very angry, pronounced, "We've got to eat him now before the big mosquitoes come."

That must have disturbed Hankie, the aussi-doodle who sleeps at the foot of my bed. His body twitched a few times and then he gave a succession of yips.

That woke him up and me as well. I'd been dreaming. I climbed out of bed and shuffled to the porch door, just to make sure that I had closed it last night. I locked it, too – something I never do. No use taking chances. Then I rubbed some more bug-juice around my ears, climbed into bed, and went back to sleep.

Staring

When we were in junior high, we had to memorize a poem by W. H. Davies called "Leisure." I didn't start the task until a few minutes before I left for school and only had a few lines down pat before English class. I finished memorization in detention after school. Now, over seven decades later, I still remember most of the lines. It begins, "What is this life if full of care, we have no time to stand and stare?" And it ends, "A poor life this if full of care, we have no time to stand and stare."

When I'm at the Little Cabin in the Big Woods, I often take the time to stand and stare. Sometimes I'm not staring at anything in particular, just letting impressions sink in. Other times, I see something really interesting that makes me focus my attention on it. Yesterday, I had a staring experience that started as the former and quickly became the latter.

I had headed down to the lake for my late afternoon dip and waded in waist deep before I stopped and began to stare. It was a very quiet afternoon, there were no boats on the water and, except for myself, the only living object seemed to be the loon chick, a brown smudge a couple of hundred feet from the shore. I watched it for a few minutes, wondering where the parent was.

Then I found out. I heard a sound in the reeds less than twenty feet from where I stood. I turned and then froze and then stared. There was the parent. The wonderful bird looked at me and then turned toward the middle of the lake and gave a ululating call. I could see her head move forward and her beak open and close as she sent a warning to her chick. She did this two or three times, each time moving a little further from the reeds. Then she pulled her head back and without opening her beak gave a long, mournful almost-howl. She moved quickly out to her chick and, staying very close to it, herded it further and further from the shore. When they were a long way off, I stopped staring and started my swim. Neither of them seemed to care.

It was a wonderful, a thrilling experience. I had never been so close to a loon before. And, although I'd heard loon calls, the birds were always in the distance. I'd never seen them making these calls. And I probably never will again. Because I'd taken time to stand and stare, my life was richer.

My father had also practiced the art of staring and here are some of the things he said about it in a column published in the *Victoria Daily Times* on July 26, 1960.

Just before we left the lake early Sunday evening, we went down to the beach, sat on the log that juts out into Cigarmakers Bay and concentrated on staring. People, I think, should do that more often. We realized that the hill we call "Old Stick" is beginning to green-up with arbutus trees edging to its peak. Pat remembers when "Stick" got its name. As a child, she saw the blackened snags that climbed to the hillcrest in sorry evidence of a bushfire that had raced through the area. The sticks have fallen now; the hillside has taken on new life. You notice it if you look—and you can see green where conifers are taking hold, too.

We looked consciously along the shore, past Copelands, by Steeles, Scotts, and Leasons. The effort was rewarding. We spend so much time bemoaning the fact that the simple joys of Shawnigan are yielding to the modern touch that we'd overlooked the obvious. New generations of children have come there. What we hadn't realized as clearly as we should have is that kids still play like kids, still find a pinnacle of triumph in their first few strokes, unaided by fins, tires, or artificial floats.

We saw, among other things, the different shadings of the trees, the color of folds in the trees, the glint and tint of water at different depths. We looked and are glad we did. We'll do it again, I hope.

Late Evening Frost

It's a chilly evening, not one for sitting outside watching the sunset, but one to light a fire inside and sink into the lazyboy. Watching TV isn't very appealing; I'm getting tired of endless analysis of the forthcoming election and of ads that explain why I shouldn't vote for a certain candidate. So I decide to read a book, but not a long novel or even a collection of short stories. I walk over to the bookshelf and pull out an old paperback I bought many years ago but haven't read in a long time: *Pocket Anthology of Robert Frost's Poems.* I could chose shorter or longer poems, and I wouldn't have to worry if I fell asleep reading one of them and forgot what it was about. It would be easy to start again at the beginning.

Robert Frost had been very important to me during my teaching career. I studied, wrote about, and taught his poems for nearly forty years. I was interested in his simple complexity, how beneath the everyday language was a subtle artistry and profound examination of human nature. Tonight, I decide to read the very short ones, the ones I best remembered, including chestnuts like "Stopping by Woods on a Snowy Evening" and "The Road Not Taken." Instead of pondering the pieces' symbolic profundities, I'd enjoy the poet's vivid, realistic presentations of moments in nature and of interactions between people.

Two of them were about chopping wood, something I'd spent some time doing in the afternoon. What delighted me were the passages that seemed to mirror my experiences and feelings. In "Two Tramps in Mud Time," the narrator describes the pleasure of cutting wood, splitting a piece cleanly: "Every piece I squarely hit / Fell splinterless as a cloven rock." That only happens to me occasionally, but it is a wonderful feeling. In "The Woodpile," he tells of discovering a bunch of logs that were cut and stacked years earlier and were now decaying. When I take a narrow two-track not far from my woodpile, I see and have seen for several years, a pyramid of eight-foot longs, gathering moss and, each year, sinking deeper into the ground.

I've read several poems, and the fire is dying down. It's time to call it an evening. But before I do, I decide to look over the table of contents again and put little checkmarks beside the ones I'd like to read at during my next fireside session. A title leaps out at me: here is a poem I must have read at one time or another, but I don't remember it. However, the title said that I had to read it now, before I hit the hay: "Blueberries." Chopping kindling and starter pieces is one of my pleasurable summer activities, but picking berries is my favorite.

The poem is in the form of a conversation between two people, probably husband and wife, and their reactions to one of them discovering the first ripe blueberries of the summer. "You ought to have seen what I saw on my way/To the village…/Blueberries as big as the end of your thumb, /Real sky blue and heavy…" That is the excitement I feel when I first see a bush full of ripe berries. A while later, they talk to a neighbor from whom one of them had asked directions to a field plentiful with berries. The neighbor replies that he had seen a patch, but the berries were all gone, and, turning to his wife, he says that they don't know of any other places. Just like me, when I am asked about my secret berry patch and give vague answers, or when, as I'm picking, somebody drives down the rutted two track and asks how it's going. I tell them that it's nearing the end of the season and that I'm going to be lucky to get enough to make batch of muffins.

When I taught poetry, especially to first-year students, many were resistant to and uninterested in what one of them called my "reading between the lines." But a few of them got almost excited when we got to Frost. "That's exactly the way I feel when I'm chopping wood or picking apples, or wandering through the woods," one of them told me. "He's just describing how he feels, not looking for some hidden meaning." I'm sure there is hidden meaning, and I don't regret having spent all those years reading between the lines. But tonight, I understand what the reluctant student had felt. In the old favorites and the one I'd forgotten, Robert Frost was describing how I've felt several times this summer.

Learning to Swim

Here's how my father described my cousin Mary's learning to swim.

My small friend Mary, who is five, has climbed her peak on Everest. She has learned to swim. At present, she propels herself a distance of five or six feet with a determined dog-paddle. Given good weather, by the end of the month she'll go from the jetty [a rock pile at one end of our little swimming bay] to the log [at the other end], a distance of around fifty feet.

Sometime in the next two or three seasons, she'll make it from the island, 300 yards away, to the shore. That is for the future. Right now, being able to swim, and never mind the distance, is the most exciting thing Mary can remember, Christmas not excluded. She learned on this week's hot Wednesday, when her father, whom she calls by his first name, was in town on business. It cost the lady who taught her a brightly burned back, but it was a small price for the triumph. "When

Wes comes," she explained to her teacher, "I'll walk out in the water with you. He'll say, 'Careful, Mary! Careful! Careful! You're getting out deep. Wait till I get your tire.' Then I'll swim. Won' 'e be surprised?" And she danced with delight.

So her father came home and was carefully coached before he walked to the beach. The five-year-old greeted him with assumed casualness and waded out. "Careful, Mary! Careful!" called the well-rehearsed parent. "Wait till I get your tire." And Mary crouched down, pushed off into a glide and began her dog-paddle. By and large, it was reasonably good theatre all around. But the casual air of the young swimmer couldn't last. "Lookit, Wes! Lookit! I can swim. I can swim," she shouted, and, in her excitement, went under. She was still bubbling happily, with water pouring out of her mouth and nose, when her teacher pulled her up and led her to shore.

Maybe there are more important accomplishments recognizable to the mind of a small child than learning to swim. If there are, they have escaped me. And to almost any adult, the memory stays fresh and green. In time, a much older Mary will be telling the folks, "When I was five, up at Shawnigan...." That's for recollection in the years ahead. Now, the fact is that she can swim—and it's as important as conquering outer space, as exciting and impressive as if no one had ever learned to swim before.

Victoria Daily Times, July 24, 1959

Reunions

Some of the most enjoyable activities at the lake are the reunions with fellow summer residents. It reminds me of the days we used to go to Andrew's hockey games. We sat with the same group of parents, occasionally went out for an after-game snack, and gathered together at the post-season awards banquet. Then we wouldn't see them again until next October when the hockey season began. In between periods and when we weren't watching the game, we'd all catch up on each other's summer.

Many of our Crooked Lake neighbors we see every summer, others every couple of years or so. We stop along the trail, sit at the dock enjoying a morning coffee or a late afternoon libation and catch up. Now that most of us are getting older, most of the conversations are about the activities of an increasing number of grandchildren, and, now that many of us are well into retirement, what we did as snowbirds during the winter.

Over the years, one of our favorite reunions has been with a family we met while camping at Colwell Lake in the early 1970s. Fred and Wanda, their five children, and their friend Dick had had discovered this wonderful camping ground almost by accident and, like us, had never camped anywhere else. I first met them during the summer of the quite unsuccessful fishing expedition Andrew and I had taken. My son and I had decided to make one further try at catching breakfast, but had discovered that our lines were totally tangled. Fred saw us struggling and helped us out.

We enjoyed many visits/reunions over the years and often over evening campfires had long pseudo-philosophical discussions. There are many memories, but two stand out. The first happened in 1985, when we'd come out from Edmonton. Years later, I jokingly blamed Mike, Fred's youngest son, for what happened. Clare had brought her BFF, who'd never gone camping and was appalled when she discovered there was no electricity, no showers, and only pit toilets. There was one only thing she liked—Mike, who was fifteen, blond, and a high school football star. The problem was, so did Clare. The two BFFs had a spat and the next day, while the friend sulked in the tent, Clare decided that she and I, along with Craig and Jan who were visiting, should go for a walk down what is now called "Crooked Lake Drive." We saw a for sale sign, and the rest is history. But what if Mike and his family hadn't been camping at the same time? And what if the two girls, who quickly became former BFFs, hadn't developed crushes on him? Would I be here today in the Little Cabin in the Big Woods?

The second happened in the late 1990s. Mary and her husband, Kevin, who had no children, showed up with four children ages three to eight. They'd wanted to adopt and had travelled to Columbia the previous winter, intending to come home with two youngsters. They returned to Michigan with four. They'd adopted an entire family! Over the next few years, when we'd have our reunions, I'd watched the children grow up. They loved Colwell Lake, and, as Marta, one of the girls once told me, "It's my favorite place in the whole world."

I've always made it a point to cruise through the campground during the Fourth of July week, when Fred and Wanda's expanding family and Dick would usually arrive. But after our 2017 reunion, I didn't see them again. I'd arrived too late or departed too early. Last year and this, I regularly cruised the campsite in early July, but none of the family was there. Perhaps they'd stopped coming to Colwell Lake. I was sorry. The annual reunions would be no more. They were part of a quickly receding past.

I felt sad, until tonight. I'd had just finished dinner at the Jackpine, a nearby restaurant, and was leaving when I heard someone call my name—something that doesn't often happen to me in the UP. It was Mary, Kevin, and Dick. It turned out that they'd switched their vacation time to early August a few years ago, and that's why I'd missed them.

There were joyous handshakes and hugs. They told me that they too had been looking every year for Clare and me, that the children they adopted, along with several of the grandchildren and great grandchildren of Fred and Wanda (who had passed away) were at the campgrounds. We arranged to get together for a reunion tomorrow.

They say you can't escape your past. And tonight I'm feeling very happy that that's the case. What a joyous day tomorrow will be.

History and a Walk to the Creek

For many years, one of our favorite morning walks has been the mile-long stroll from the Little Cabin in the Big Woods to the bridge crossing the south branch of Stutts Creek. It was a pleasant but routine walk: the dogs had their favorite places to sniff; when we heard a vehicle approaching, I'd yell "car" like the kids playing street hockey and we'd all dive into the bushes; occasionally a squirrel would scoot across the road and the dogs would pull hard on their leashes. One time, I got brave and followed an overgrown road past a "Private Property" sign and discovered a bunch of old, abandoned, rusting cars, trucks, and even a snowplow. Apparently that's the way a long-ago resident, one of the pioneers of Crooked Lake, used to get rid of his broken down vehicles.

But the sense of the walk's routineness vanished this winter. Several years ago, before the ferns had grown tall enough to conceal it, I'd noticed a very large white pine stump in the woods just opposite our driveway. Judging from its diameter, the tree had probably been over two hundred years old when it was felled in the late nineteenth century. That would have meant that before Father Marquette had explored the Upper Peninsula in the 1660s, the tree was a healthy sapling. It was fun to imagine what people and animals had passed by it—missionaries, surveyors, and timber cruisers, bear and deer, maybe even moose or cougars before they became scarce in the neighborhood. How many fires had it survived before it felt the bite of a logger's axe or the ripping of a crosscut saw? And were any of the much smaller pines around the stump its descendants?

Then this winter, I bought a copy of the 70th anniversary reprint of William S. Crowe's *Lumberjack: Inside an Era in the Upper Peninsula of Michigan.* On the cover was a very old photograph of some men poling logs along a "river." The river was Stutts Creek. The sleepy, lazy stream that flows under the bridge had an important place in the history of this part of the Upper Peninsula. During the autumn it would have been groomed, cleared of trees that had fallen in it and would be dangerous obstructions during the spring drive. Dams would be built at intervals along it to raise the level of the water to ensure as smooth a passage as possible of the logs. The dams would be opened (perhaps blasted open) and the logs would go through to the next dam. The Stutts creek would empty the winter's harvest into the Manistique River and the logs would arrive at mills in Manistique, be turned into lumber, loaded onto ships destined for southern Great Lakes' ports, and then reloaded onto rail cars and sent to the rapidly expanding Midwest to be turned into buildings.

Now, as we make the morning stroll to the bridge, I have a new set of imaginings. Perhaps the two track that the dogs and I amble along had been one of the ice roads, made so by their nightly spraying of water from a zamboni-like machine, along which felled logs were pulled. That would be the first stage of the journey of a majestic white pine that had grown up behind what is now our cabin.

I wonder if somewhere in Illinois or Iowa there's an old, decrepit cabin or an old, leaning barn that has lumber from our tree. If the boards could talk, they could tell a story of an amazing journey.

Logging Some Calories

Fig. 5-2: Eight feet long and close to three feet in diameter, this log in front of the Tahquamenon Falls Logging Museum is a reminder of the size of the trees nineteenth-century loggers had to fell.

Well-maintained equipment and warm clothing were two of the essentials for the loggers who worked in the Upper Peninsula. AND good food and plenty of it. The cook may have been one of the most important people in a logging camp. If you criticized him, you were in danger of being gone. If he did not provide good, hot, nourishing food, food loaded with proteins and carbohydrates, he stood a good chance of being gone. A good breakfast was a must. Going into the woods in the predawn darkness, working for twelve hours in brutal cold was no easy task. The fuel needed to complete it included pancakes, biscuits, fried potatoes, beans, sow-belly (salt pork), and occasionally ham, bacon, and venison sausages. There might be dried prunes or apples. All of this was washed down with black tea.

How important the food was to these men was reflected in the stories they told. There was no talking in the cook shack. They had to eat fast and get out so that the flunkies (cook's helpers) could clean the place and start preparing another meal. Moreover, given the many nationalities found in most logging camps, talks might lead to quarrels and fights. But back in the bunk house, they could spin yarns. They told stories about frying pans so big that the flunkies would strap slabs of bacon on their boots and skate around greasing the pans. There was another story about a flunky who was so dumb that he put a cup of dynamite into the biscuit mix instead of baking powder and nearly blew the cook shack away. One of the cooks liked to put beans in nearly everything and the loggers complained bitterly. The noises from several of the sleeping men kept the others awake at night. Often it was necessary to open the windows, even in sub-zero weather. The frigid air was better than that inside.

The great pine logging era is long over. But visitors to the Upper Peninsula can get a taste of what it was like—literally. Several Saturdays and Sundays during the summer, fifteen volunteers from the Tahquamenon Falls Logging Museum Society work to create an all-you-can-eat logger's breakfast that includes pancakes (with butter and syrup), eggs, sausages, bacon, and potatoes. There's coffee and milk to wash it down, along with orange juice, something that certainly wasn't available to members of Paul Bunyan's crew. The price is only twelve dollars a person.

On a recent Saturday, we made the trip from the Little Cabin in the Big Woods to Newberry, the location of the museum in which the feast was held. Inside a replica of a log-sided cook house, people sat at picnic tables, chatting and laughing, happily ignoring the "No Talking During Meals" sign. The meal was great and the decorations on the walls very interesting. On one side, five large circular saws contained paintings depicting different logging eras. Above the kitchen hung blue enamelware pots, pans, and bowls, along with cast iron fry pans. Old logging equipment—crosscut saws, a yoke for two oxen, and other equipment—adorned another wall. And, finally, on a fourth wall hung two pairs of long johns, essential winter garments. They were spotless and in excellent repair, and one was pink! They obviously weren't museum pieces. I'll bet they were ordered from Amazon.

After such a nourishing and filling meal, most of us had no room for seconds, although I did go back for a couple of pieces of bacon and a glass of orange juice. We walked (waddled?) around the museum buildings. There were historical photographs, copies of very old magazine articles, and really interesting lumbering artifacts. I was most interested in the logging tools—the crosscuts, axes, bucksaws, peavies, and pike poles. When I was growing up along the Vancouver Island waterfront over seven decades ago, my grandfather had similar tools he'd used for gathering driftwood (and occasionally a log that had broken away from a boom) and then sawing and splitting it. In my mind, I had made a trip back to Michigan's logging past, to the days of my adolescent appetite, and to my grandfather's favorite retirement activity.

I was glad there was a designated driver on the hour-and-a-half drive back to Crooked Lake. Most of us were dozing off. Now that I'm back at the cabin, I think I'm going to have to work off some calories. There are logs to be split and kindling chopped, because tomorrow morning is going to be chilly. First, I think I need a good afternoon nap. I know that I won't be having much for dinner. I'm not the trencherman I used to be.

DIRECTIONS: From the intersection of M-28 and M-123, take M-123 North through and a mile past Newberry. The Tahquamenon Falls Logging Museum is on the left.

Blueberries for Ale

Earlier this week, I spent a half hour or so checking over one of the appendices for *Yooper Ale Trails*, a book about the craft breweries of the Upper Peninsula. "A guide to beer styles" included descriptions of several dozen styles followed by a list of examples of each style produced by the breweries of Michigan's UP. Not surprisingly, the most popular style is India Pale Ale, with well over four dozen IPAs—West Coast, East Coast, and one called "No Coast," Imperials and session ales -- brewed above the Bridge. What was surprising was the second most popular style: the loosely-defined category of "fruit beers," with forty-three listed.

The most popular fruit additive is blueberries, with two dozen beers on the list. It's been called the "National Beer of the UP." Kyle Peterson, then the brewer at Lake Superior Smokehouse Brewpub, once told me, "We're not allowed to not have it." According to Jeff Brickey, owner-brewer of 51st State Brewing, "When we started it, I put Batty Millie on our list just so we'd have something for people new to craft beer or for people who don't like beer. Now it's our top seller. One day, a guy came in and, when he found it wasn't on tap, he walked out in a huff."

The history of the Upper Peninsula's blueberry beers goes back to the mid-1990s, when the craft beer movement first arrived above the Bridge. Derek "Chumley" Anderson, of Marquette Harbor Brewery at Vierling Restaurant, and Lark Ludlow, of Tahquamenon Falls Brewery and Restaurant, worked together to create a Blueberry Wheat Ale for the annual Blueberry Festival held in the small village of Paradise. A few weeks later, Chumley introduced a similar beer for Marquette's Blueberry Festival.

Like these originals, most of the UP's blueberry ales use American wheat ale as the base beer. It's a medium-bodied, not-at-all overpowering beer that allows the subtle fruit hints created by the blueberry puree to shine. "It's like spreading a thin layer of blueberry jelly on a thick slice of fresh homemade bread," one brewer told me.

Other base beers are used as well: Kolsch for Cold Iron's Blue Collar Blueberry (which doesn't use puree but freshly-picked blueberries which are smooshed, cooked, and added to the beer during secondary fermentation), and Berliner Weisse, a gently sour German beer, for Ore Dock's Blue Canoe, to name but two. And there are other additives as well; 51st State's Batty Millie adds vanilla; Hereford & Hops, lemon grass; and Cognition's Pombluegenesis, pomegranates.

The wild blueberry season in the Upper Peninsula only lasts for a few weeks during the summer. Soo Brewing celebrates the beginning of that oh-so-short-time by releasing its Crystal Blue Persuasion on the day of the summer solstice. But many UP breweries always have their blueberry beers on tap, keeping the memory of summer alive all year.

Two of the most unusual blueberry beers are, unfortunately, brewed in towns two hours apart and one of them comes out in the late spring and the other after Labor Day. ByGeorge Brewing of Munising is the maker of Batter UP! Blueberry and Maple Syrup Pancake Pilsner; Cognition of Ishpeming puts out its Phasmosis Ghost Cereal Gose as one of its spooky Halloween releases. Added to the grist is an unspecified amount of a popular blueberry-flavored breakfast cereal. (From the name you can probably guess what the cereal is.)

It would be fun, I often think, to have a growler of each in my fridge and to enjoy a glass of each while hunkering down to a hearty morning meal of ham and eggs or flapjacks well-coated with butter.

That would certainly be a breakfast of champions!

Turn! Turn! Turn!

Fig. 5-3: As the summer wanes, an occasional branch of red leaves serves as a reminder that autumn will soon arrive.

In the wee small hours, it was so cold that I shut the window and got out a heavy quilt to put over the bed. The dawn's early light didn't creep over the windowsill until nearly seven, over an hour later than in June. The temperature on the indoor-outdoor thermometer read 45 degrees outside, the lowest in two months.

It was too cold to sit on the screened porch to enjoy morning coffee, so I lit a fire, watched the flames and listened to the coffee splashing into the glass pot. The hummingbird did not drive an interloper, maybe one of this year's offspring, away from the feeder. Perhaps both were bulking up getting ready for their long journey south. The robin was nowhere to be seen. A full moon, what the Anishinaabe called the moon of the wild rice, set across the lake.

The sun rose above the eastern tree line, its rays coloring the western tree line with pale gold. The maples and birches had lost their full rich greenness of July. The rays then infused the gray mist with a weak yellow tinge. The water was warmer than the air, although a later check of the water thermometer revealed that the lake was eight degrees cooler than it had been at noon yesterday.

After the mist had burned off, three adult loons flew low over the water, landed briefly, and then taxied off to the north. Perhaps they were from another lake and were having a brief rest before resuming their trip south. Shortly after, the resident loon and its chick came by. The chick was almost as big as the parent, had developed white adult markings on its chest, and dove regularly in search of breakfast.

In the middle of the back road, a fresh pile of coyote scat had red, unripe blackberries in it. The bracken that had sprung up so suddenly in late May had begun to brown and wither. A branch of a maple tree had turned a brilliant red. There were purple asters where the daisies had bloomed a month ago.

Before lunch, I took a short canoe trip, paddling and then drifting along the shore. Outdoor chairs had disappeared from many of the docks and fewer colorful kayaks were pulled up on the bank. Spires of goldenrod bloomed along the banks. From cabins set back in the trees, smoke drifted from chimneys. Some residents had kept their morning fires going.

Later in the afternoon, on the way out to the mailbox to pick up today's paper, I took a spin through the campground. Over half the sites were empty and in many of the others, people huddled around campfires. When I got home and opened the paper, a back-to-school flier slipped out. The evening news carried several back-to-school stories.

Before nine, the sun, which in June had set far to the north behind two giant white pines shortly after ten, began to sink behind smaller trees near the south tip of "Mewinzha Peninsula," the point of land directly across the lake from the Little Cabin in the Big Woods. The rays glinted off the small waves created by a chilly, freshening breeze from the north and turned the trunks of the birches beside the cabin into pale gold pillars.

When the darkness moved in, turning the lake from a dappled, Monet-like tapestry to a purple and then black velvet blanket, I retreated to the cabin and lit a small fire. The eleven-o'clock news reported that the temperature tonight would be even colder than it was last night and to take any potted plants inside. I exchanged my pajamas for a pair of long johns, closed the window tightly, and called the two dogs up on the bed so that they would keep me warm.

As I drifted to sleep, the words from the Pete Seeger/ Byrds' song ran through my mind. "To everything there is a season." Like my avian co-tenants, I knew that summer was almost over.

Soon it will be time to go.

August 25th, 1993

We closed camp on this date in 1993. It had been a difficult summer, the first we'd spent at the Little Cabin in the Big Woods since we'd lost Carol. My twin sister, Sheri, and her husband, Eugene, had joined Clare and me for our last week at the lake. We picked blueberries, drank a toast to what would have been Carol's and my thirtieth wedding anniversary, and shared memories of the times long ago when Sheri and I had spent our summers at Shawnigan Lake on Canada's West Coast.

The day before we departed, Sheri and Eugene back to Victoria and me to Edmonton (Clare had flown back to Edmonton a couple of days earlier), Sheri and I baked a batch of muffins that were chock full of blueberries we'd picked a couple of days earlier. The day after she and Eugene got home, they were going to take a box filled with them up to Shawnigan for my mother and father to enjoy.

I dropped them of at the Marquette airport and began the long drive west to Edmonton. When I arrived at the first night's motel, the clerk gave me the message all travelers dread: "Call home right away." I reached Andrew, who told me that my father had passed away in the morning. While I was driving across the Upper Peninsula, feeling a little melancholy that another summer was nearly over, my father had had his breakfast and headed outside, as he routinely did, to do some small chores. He had gone down to the lake to move some rather large rocks along the shore. However, soon he walked up to the house complaining of a stomach ache and telling my mother that he was going to lie down for a while. A few minutes later, he died of an abdominal aneurism.

This morning, three decades later, as I sipped my morning coffee and watched the mist rising from the lake, I thought about my father and how much he had loved the retirement years he had spent beside his lake. I would shape my day's activities around my memories of him and his activities.

Breakfast over, I took my morning canoe ride, practicing the techniques and etiquette of paddling he had taught me. As the canoe glided through the water, I softly sang the words to "The Whiffenpoof Song," one he used to sing to his three tired children as they dozed in the back seat of the car heading back to town after a weekend at the lake. At my father's memorial celebration, held beside Shawnigan Lake, his grandson Charlie played that song on his saxophone, bringing tears to the eyes of my mother, my sisters, and me.

As he used to, I spent much of the morning doing simple outside chores. Today, I cleared and roughed up the space in front of the Little Cabin in the Big Woods and then cast wildflower seeds over it. They would be in bloom when Clare and I came back to Crooked Lake in ever-returning spring. It was time for lunch and an afternoon nap, a habit I'd inherited from him. I did a few more chores after the sleep, the most important being the chopping of kindling and starter pieces of wood. The temperature could to drop this evening and a small fire would bring a cheery glow to the cabin as the darkness set in.

In the summer, gin and tonic was his favorite happy hour drink and, late this afternoon, the day's work done, I sipped one on the dock of the bay thinking of so many things he had done for me during my life.

In the evenings, my father enjoyed lighting a small fire and, as the world outside darkened, he'd gaze into the flames and then embers, musing, meditating and remembering. It turned out to be too warm this evening to make a fire, so I sat on the screened porch, and, in the quietness interrupted only by the whir of the hummingbird at the feeder and the distant churr of a squirrel, I watched the golden rays of the setting sun shine through the trees. I too mused, meditated, and remembered.

As the sun turned from gold to vermillion, I thought of two wonderful gifts he had bequeathed to me: a love of the simple things of life and the joy of discovering words to describe them. His gifts continue to nourish me and enrich my life.

Along the Boardwalk — Manistique

There's a story, perhaps apocryphal, that the nineteenth-century New England writers Hawthorne and Thoreau were walking along a woodland path when the former expressed admiration for his companion's ability to see so many things during a simple stroll. "You have to know what you're looking for," Thoreau responded. "And you have to keep your eyes on the ground." He then bent over and picked an old arrowhead out of the dust.

Fig. 5-4: The Manistique Boardwalk, which extends two miles along the shore of Lake Michigan, is the home to a variety of small ecosystems.

I thought about that story this morning when I made my final excursion of the season, a late August walk along Manistique's boardwalk, which lies between Highway 2 and the northern Lake Michigan shore and extends eastward for almost two miles from the banks of the Manistique River. My guide was Deb LeBlanc, whose photographs grace this book and who is a retired botanist for the U.S. Forest Service. She keeps her eyes on the ground and she knows what to look for. The boardwalk (actually a boardwalk and concrete trail) passes through a natural area that ranges from 100 to 300 yards wide and contains several small ecosystems: the shoreline, the beach, sand dunes, swales (wetland areas between sand dunes), and more sand dunes. Each ecosystem has its own characteristics and flora and fauna.

We'd walked the full length of the boardwalk earlier in the season. Today, we were going to go from the parking lot just across from the old Forest Service building for a half-a-mile and then back, both of us keeping our eyes on the ground. Deb, who created the text for the many interpretative signs along the way, pointed things out to me and then explained what she had noticed,. She spotted well over two dozen plant species during our hour-long stroll.

Just as we left the parking lot, I pointed out one of the few flowering plants I recognized. "Is that spotted knapweed?" I asked. She answered in the affirmative and explained that it was an invasive species that made the ground in which it grew so toxic that native plants couldn't survive there. Then, she pointed to a plant just behind me, one I hadn't noticed. It was beach pea, a native plant that was edible. She drew my attention to the pods and said that they tasted like snap peas.

Most of the plants she drew my attention to were late bloomers, the flowers of late August and September. These included wormwood, only found on the dunes; the goldenrod that is seen at this time of year almost everywhere there's sunshine; and another species of goldenrod, Houghton's goldenrod. It's endangered, protected by state law, and it's distinguished by the fact that the blooms form a crown or umbrella at the top of the stalk. It is only seen along the shorelines of the Great Lakes

We took a brief detour off the trail onto the limestone-covered beach where we saw lobelia, white boneset (which only grows close to the shore), and potentilla (which requires alkaline soil). We also saw the shells of zebra mussels, those tiny invasive creatures that have so devastated the waters and shores of the Great Lakes.

Back on the trail, I was gazing at an old apple tree (perhaps there had once been a farm here) and eastern white cedars laden with cones, when Deb warned, "Watch where you're stepping." I thought for a moment that I was in danger of crushing an endangered plant. But what I just missed was planting my boot on a pile of bear poop. I knew what that was, having occasionally seen some not far from the cabin. Ever the naturalist, Deb explained that, judging from the size of the scat, it was probably a young bear and that it had recently had a meal of wild cherries. The evidence was the presence of small pits in the scat.

We had almost reached the turning point in our stroll when Deb exclaimed: "Look, fringed gentian. I was hoping we'd see some." Just at the edge of the beach was a clump of beautiful, bell-shaped flowers. Hardy plants that thrive in rocky soil, they bloom from later summer well into autumn. I'd never seen them before. They certainly were the most beautiful autumn blossoms I'd ever encountered.

As I gazed, I recalled several poems I'd read about them, perhaps the most famous by American poets William Cullen Bryant, Emily Dickinson, and Robert Frost. In "To the Fringed Gentian," Bryant, writing in the early nineteenth century, expressed great admiration of the flower, saying it gave him hope about facing the winter in his life. Emily Dickinson's "God Made a Little Gentian" recounts how the flower had been overshadowed in summer but had achieved grandeur in the autumn when the others had faded. Frost, in "The Quest of the Purple-Fringed," described a long hike made to discover the season's first gentian. Having found it, he accepted the fact that "summer was done."

Having this beautiful flower pointed out to me by someone who knew what she was looking for, seeing it for the first time, marked a wonderful ending to the last excursion of my summer. To many, the beauty of autumn is in the colors of the dying leaves. They are beautiful. But the flowers of the fringed gentians are exquisite—they speak of the continuing life of autumn.

DIRECTIONS: For nearly two miles east from the junction of Michigan Highway 94 and US Highway 2 there are several clearly-marked parking lots on the south side of US 2.

Clouds Overhead ... A Cloud Over My Head

This year, Labor Day is almost three weeks before the official end of summer, the Autumnal Equinox. But in my childhood, and now, in my second childhood, it marks the end of summer. The week before it was and is one of the saddest of the year. No matter what the weather at Shawnigan Lake, my siblings, my cousins, and I would walk around like Joe Btfsplk, the woebegone character in the L'il Abner comic strip who always had a cloud hovering over his head. In my second childhood, I still do.

Long ago, the week before Labor Day started badly. On the Sunday night, my sisters and I had to go back to Victoria. "It isn't fair," we'd mutter. Our cousins got to stay at the lake. But there were so many back-to-school things to be done. We'd go to buy new clothes. (Unlike my sisters, I was quite happy to wear the old broken-in ones—I hadn't grown much in the summer.) I had to be shorn of the Tarzan-length locks I'd grown over the summer, and I was marched to the neighbor-hood barber shop. (At least he had a really good collection of comic books.) We had to tidy our closets and our little desks, all of which had acquired a great volume of summer-time clutter.

Our father would drive us back to the lake after he'd finished work on Wednesday. We'd swim, play parking-lot baseball, and listen to "The Lone Ranger" on my grandmother's big battery-powered radio. But a listless melancholy hung over us like Joe Btfsplk's cloud. The cousins would be leaving on Saturday and Sunday. On Monday, Sheri, Gael, and I would help lift the kayak into storage and then tidy up and pack the books and toys, paper and crayons that had kept us amused on rainy days. We'd be back to the lake for the occasional fall weekends, but these visits wouldn't be the same: summer was over.

This week, the closing up will be different. It will be final; no weekend visits. The day after Labor Day, I won't be trudging three blocks to school. I'll begin the 1900 mile, four-and-a-half day drive to the City of the Pavements Gray.

Opening in May, just before Memorial Day, the unofficial beginning of summer, had been a joyous occasion. Groceries, clothes, and books had been quickly unloaded from the car and put away. Then began a few days of rituals celebrating my return to the Little Cabin in the Big Woods: the first craft beer sipped on the dock; the first dinner, always a pasty; cleaning up the mice's winter leavings; raking the autumn leaves away from the house; the first swim; and the first canoe expedition.

This week's activities will be necessary routines, not ritual celebrations. Monday, I'll make a detailed list of tasks that I must not forget to do. There's no turning back when you cross the Interstate Bridge that separates the Upper Peninsula from Wisconsin. Tuesday, I'll put stops on newspaper and postal deliveries and telephone and internet services and will make reservations for the motels I'll stay at along the way. Wednesday, there'll be a trip to town to do laundry (we'll want clean sheets and cabin clothes when we return in the spring) and pick up a few basic things to keep the dogs and me from starving before we leave. Thursday is the time to pack up the clothes, books, and non-perishable foods that won't be needed this week, and will go back to Albuquerque

Friday, the closing up chores begin in earnest: chopping starter wood and kindling and storing it in the shed in preparation for spring's arrival; straightening up and tidying the cabin room by room, checking that no items that need to be taken with us are overlooked.

The weekend is the hardest part. The loveseat that Carol and I bought decades ago is dragged up from the dock. The canoe that had been paddled on so many wonderful quiet and calm mornings is hauled out of the water. These are pulled up to the screen porch, where we enjoyed our mosquito-free evenings. The porch itself has been turned into a storage room, with the table, easy chairs, lamps and benches piled in a corner to make room for canoe and loveseat. There is nowhere left to sit and enjoy morning coffee while gazing at the lake.

Of course, it would be nice if the weather were sunny and warm all week, although the forecast is for some rain in a couple of days. But, if there are clouds and rain, they will be a perfect complement to the Btfsplk cloud that has hovered over me all week.

My grown children often tell me, when they think I'm over exerting myself, "Remember, you're not the kid you once were." But, as I think of the week ahead and remember the Labor Day week blues of long ago, I think I still am.

I wish that darn cloud would quit hovering over my head!

6   Labor Day Weekend – The End of a Season

It's supposed to be the last hurrah of the summer season. But for most of us at the lake, it's a time of melancholy, of packing up and closing down, of one last swim or morning canoe excursion or walk along the lakeshore. There's a reluctance to accept the end of the season, a reluctance that is only slightly lessened by the realization that in another eight months, the lake will be the scene of ever-returning spring.

Saturday: Walking Around Colwell Lake

Fig 6-1: The goldenrods along the lakeside trail are symbols of the golden memories gathered during the soon-to-end "Wild Blueberry Summer"

In 1971, we spent our first Labor Day weekend in the Upper Peninsula, camping at Colwell Lake. The weather was ideal: afternoon temperatures in the upper seventies, sunny days, and no mosquitoes. We set up at site 15, and soon Andrew and Clare were paddling and splashing in the water. Andrew, much to his mother's alarm, shimmied up a long and very thick branch hanging over the water. In the evening we toasted marshmallows over a campfire. One day we hiked around the lake on a narrow little footpath that had plenty of fallen logs to step over and branches hanging above the trail ready to slap an inattentive walker in the face.

Today, fifty-three Labor Day weekends later, I hiked the path again. For over two decades, it's been a wide, well-groomed trail with crushed gravel stretches and boardwalks over marshy areas. It wouldn't be the same as the long-ago walk: we had lost Carol many years ago; Clare was in New Mexico, and Andrew in Alberta. My stroll, just over three miles, would be both a sentimental journey and a re-education about the lives and deaths of trees.

As I walked along the first couple of hundred yards, I became both angry and sad. A private logging company had all but clear-cut a grove of maples, leaving only those that were too immature to be harvested and a bunch of alders that were of no commercial use. In some cases, the loggers had cut trees on both sides of the trail, in places closer than twenty feet from rustic campsites. Slash littered the forest floor, creating what could and probably would become a serious fire hazard. In the campground, many signs tell the campers to clean up after themselves. Evidently these rules don't apply to logging companies.

The rest of the "journey" was much less stressful. There were many downed trees, but they had died naturally—from age and disease, or from being snapped off up the trunks or uprooted during strong winds. Except where trunks had blocked the trail, they had been left where they had fallen, on land or in the water, where they would play roles in the nourishing of new life.

One of the benches that are placed every couple or so hundred yards along the trail faced toward the forest, not the water, as the others did. I used to think this placement was unusual, but as I sat on the bench, I understood why it faced the way it did. It looked at the full variety of the forest. There were evergreens, maples and aspens, tall trees and short ones, trees living and dead. Out of one decaying stump, a reminder of a logging era of over a century ago, a maple sapling rose.

"Enjoy it while you can," I said, remembering the devastation I'd seen a few minutes earlier.

As the trail passed by the campsites, many scenes reminded me of the visits we'd made as a young family. A few people had put chairs in the water and were reading or just gazing, as Carol used to. On the bank front of Site 15 lay a very thick, eight-foot long log, all that was left of the branch Andrew had so precariously perched on five decades earlier. A few sites past number 15, a long fishing pier extended into the lake. Perhaps if it had been there in the 1970s, Andrew and I might have been more successful anglers. A few hundred feet further, I stopped at the swimming beach/picnic area. Here, forty years ago, Clare and a friend had had their spat over a handsome teenage camper.

My sentimental stroll around Colwell Lake completed, I returned to the cabin. It had been a fine Labor Day Saturday. I had seen the natural world at its best (and, briefly, worst). And I had recovered memories that were as bright and warming as the goldenrods that blossomed along the lake shore.

Sunday: While I Was Sleeping ...

August turned into September ... a brief, but fierce storm from the north, the first of the fall season, swept down the lake. I didn't know about it until the next morning, when I saw branches littering the two-track behind the Little Cabin in the Big Woods. Then I understood why Katrina, who usually sleeps in the hall, had joined Hankie on the bed, leaving me clinging to its edge ... when I did awake, the temperature inside was well below sixty and, for the first time in a while I turned on the baseboard heaters ... the high was only going to be 64 degrees, twenty lower than yesterday ... a strong wind continued blowing from the north, creating whitecaps that seemed to be racing to the south end of the lake ... all morning, the wind kept the trees swaying dangerously ... the lights flickered briefly, then they went out completely as I was just about sit down at the computer .... Deb arrived to collect the food I wasn't going to take home. I opened the fridge door quickly and pulled things out, because I didn't want my happy hour beer to get warm ... inside the cabin, the temperature dropped into the fifties, so I lit a fire then called Patty, the neighbor down the way, to see if anyone had called the power company. She then told me they had, and also that she'd discovered six snakes behind her futon—were they cold?

The power came back on, but it was too cold to take a dip or sit on the porch enjoy a beer, so I warmed my pasty (the last summer dinner I traditionally cook for myself), had dinner, did some more packing and took some boxes to the car. It was getting colder outside and I thought about that Rachel Field poem, "Something told the wild geese it was time to go"—and, for those six snakes, "time to come inside." For me, too and so I did... I put another log on the fire and read some autumn poems by Robert Frost ...That night as I drifted off, I remembered a line from one of Shakespeare's sonnets: "Summer's lease hath all too short a date."

Monday: Memory Trees

Earlier this evening, after the summer's final get-together with the neighbors, a fish-fry hosted by Rick and Betsy, I took the last walk of the season along the shoreline. The narrow footpath, which is only a few yards from the shore, passes through stands of trees that reflect the arboreal variety and history of our woodlands. There are very large stumps left from the late nineteenth century white-pine logging era; along the shore there are cedar stumps, some of which still show where axes and crosscut saws were used to harvest timber and some of which bear the marks of forest fires that passed through

Fig. 6-2: A dead hemlock that hugs the bank is a memorial to one who dearly loved the Little Cabin in the Big Woods

the area. There are tiny seedlings, young saplings, and a few forest giants—white pines that were sufficiently deformed to survive the logging era. There are dead logs of birch that had finished their relatively short lives (around eighty years) and fallen to the ground where their decaying trunks provide nourishment for other living beings. I must have walked by over a dozen species of trees whose ages ranged from one year to well over a hundred.

I've probably walked this lakeside path at least five hundred times in the nearly forty years I've been at the Little Cabin in the Big Woods, and the trees and their predecessors have become so familiar that I don't usually pay close attention to them. They are old friends, and we share this edge of this little lake, each of us living our own lives.

But this evening I paused and looked carefully at two trees: a blue spruce sapling and a dead eastern hemlock. Blue spruce trees are not native to the Upper Peninsula; they grow naturally in the Rocky Mountain States but are often raised around the country in nurseries and sold as ornamental trees. Eastern hemlocks, which bear the Latin name of psuga Canadensis and the Anishinaabe name of giizha, have been native here for at least three thousand years. Both trees are hardy, survivors in rugged growing conditions, and long-living; both have been sources of traditional medicines, both offer winter shelter to the animals with whom they share the landscape. And both the spruce and the hemlock I gazed at are very special to the people with whom they share a small portion of the lakeside landscape.

I first noticed the blue spruce a few years ago. It was set back from the path and was dwarfed and nearly concealed by the trees around it. What distinguished it were a number of photographs that had been laminated and then hung by wires on the branches. The next time I encountered Jeff, the owner of the cabin, I asked him about the tree. It was, he told me, a tribute to his mother and a brother who had died. The cabin had been one of the first built at Crooked Lake, and Jeff, his siblings and his mother had spent summers there, joined as often as possible by Jeff's father, who worked downstate.

"When my brother and my mother died, we had their ashes sprinkled here and we wanted a tree to celebrate their lives, something special, something a little different from the other evergreens here. My brother Randy, who works for the Forest Service, got us this blue spruce. We weren't sure at first if it would survive; but it has, and it's grown." The tree and the photographs perpetuate the memories of a family, four generations of which have called Crooked Lake their special place.

The other tree, an eastern hemlock, was the one in front of our place, one that we have lovingly called "The Tom Thomson Tree," a reference to a well-known painting by a major Canadian artist. It clung to the bank at the edge of the lake, leaning outward over the water, as if trying to escape the shadows created by the larger trees around it and to gather in the afternoon sunlight. The only way we knew it was growing was the fact that every couple of years we'd have to trim back a foot or so of face-high branches that used to greet us as we walked onto the dock. A couple of summers after the Little Cabin in the Big Woods had become part of our lives, I suggested that we cut it down to make it easier to slide the rowboat (which we haven't used for years) into the water. "Woodsman, spare that tree!" I remember Carol saying to me, laughingly but very seriously.

I missed a couple of years at the lake during the pandemic, and when I returned, I noticed that the Tom Thomson tree did not have the rich profusion of needles it once had. The next year, it had less, and two years ago it was dead. When a neighbor kindly offered to cut it down, I politely and firmly refused his offer and explained why. It remains a tribute to the memory of Carol, who gathered sunshine as the hemlock did and whose grace and goodness offered emotional shelter to family and friends. As the blue spruce is to Jeff and his family, so the hemlock is to Clare and me, a memorial to those we have loved.

As the rays of the setting sun streamed through the trees, I packed the final box for the trip home. It is a metaphorical box, a box of memories of a glorious summer and of days before. One little memory I put in it is of picking a small cone on the ground next to the hemlock and placing it well away from the trail. Perhaps it will become a new hemlock. Even if not, the memory of its "parent" will remain strong and hardy for us.

Tuesday: Envoi

Like kids walking to the school bus stop the day after Labor Day feeling melancholy over the end of their summer vacation, I felt a sweet sadness as I locked the doors of the Little Cabin in the Big Woods and performed the final ritual of this summer, saying goodbye to Crooked Lake. I would be taking a box of happy memories and several bags of

Fig. 6-2: This Monarch will not return, but her descendants will...

frozen blueberries back to the City of the Pavements Gray. But in just over three hours, when I had crossed the Interstate Bridge separating the Upper Peninsula and northern Wisconsin, the place for which I feel such great *querencia* would start to become long ago and far away.

My mood resembled that of the speaker in Robert Frost's poem "Reluctance." Although he was speaking about late autumn, I agreed with his sentiment: "Ah, when in the heart of man/Was it ever less than a treason… /[to] bow and accept the end/ Of a love or a season?"

As I reached the dock, I remembered another time I'd walked from the locked cabin to say good-bye to the lake. I'd been in the same kind of mood. That had changed when I saw a monarch butterfly fluttering before me. He'd begun a long journey to his winter home. He'd not return in the spring, but his descendants would, renewing the summer cycles of life and death. Earlier that day, the neighbors had walked along the path, the son of the people who had built their cabin, his wife, one of their daughters, and a grandchild. The daughter was pregnant and talked about her soon-to-be-born son making his first visit to the lake late next May.

The memory of seeing the butterfly and hearing about a new neighbor changed my mood. The English poet Shelley wrote, "If winter comes, can spring be far behind?" In northern Michigan, spring will be far behind. But it will come. Perhaps, next spring, the tiny hemlock cone I picked up from the path and placed carefully in the woods will have begun its own life cycle.

I remembered lines from another Frost poem, "The Onset." "Winter death has never tried the earth, but it has failed." I touched the dry bark of the hemlock and whispered softly, "Thanks for all the memories." As I walked past the cabin on the way to the car, I touched it as well. "I'll see you next spring," I told it. At the beginning of autumn, I felt the promise of ever-returning spring.

Epilogue: A Yooper Brunch in New Mexico

Fig. E-1: The ingredients and recipes for a Yooper brunch that, during the long months of winter, will bring back memories of the Wild Blueberry Summer

Shortly before seven in the morning, I opened the blinds of my study and looked down Eastern Avenue toward the Manzano Mountains. The Autumn Equinox had occurred a few minutes earlier and, in a couple of minutes, the sun would rise at the end of Eastern. These were moments of transition—the summer was officially ending and days of decreasing daylight were beginning. The sky above the Manzanos was roseate and, after the red orb had lifted above the skyline, it seemed that autumn had begun.

Behind me on the western wall of my study hung the three large photographs of Crooked Lake. The trees in the pictures were the rich green of summer. Now, they would be tinged with branches of scarlet and gold. The loons, the robins, and the hummingbirds would have departed In another week or so, the last of the summer residents will have closed their cabins for the season. The Little Cabin in the Big Woods seemed long ago and far away to me.

By late morning, my mood of sweet melancholy had lifted. Clare was preparing a brunch to celebrate the wonderful summer we'd spent at Crooked Lake. The principal ingredients spanned the growing seasons of the Upper Peninsula. In *ziizbaakdokegiizis*, the sugar-making moon (March), Harry Haglund, who lives a half-hour drive from Crooked Lake, had finished making maple syrup the old fashioned way. In the summer, he had gifted me with two bottles of this first product of nature's spring reawakening. The golden liquid would be poured over pancakes loaded with the wild blueberries that I had harvested in *miini-giizis*, the blueberry moon (July), at my secret blueberry patch, ten minutes away from the cabin. And the wonderful breakfast would be washed down with "Batter UP! Pilsner," the blueberry maple syrup lager that George Schultz had brewed at ByGeorge! Brewing in Munising (forty minutes away) during the blooming moon, baashkaabigonii-giizis (June). As the summer transitioned into autumn, our brunch would remind us of the golden days of our wild blueberry summer. The Little Cabin in the Big Woods wouldn't feel so long ago and far away.

That afternoon, I planned to finish my unpacking. The clothes had long ago been hung up or put in the laundry hamper, the books and notebooks taken to the study, the craft beers picked up on the long journey home put in the fridge, and the one-cup bags of wild blueberries nestled on a shelf of the freezer. The intervening weeks had been spent with appointments and household duties that had been postponed since spring. Today I would sit quietly and gently take out items from the metaphorical box of memories that I'd packed on the last evening at the lake. You could only see them with what Wordsworth called "that inner eye which is the bliss of solitude." I'd place them on a metaphorical shelf just below the three big wall pictures. And the Little Cabin in the Big Woods would feel a little closer.

The sun won't rise above the Manzanos at the end of Eastern Avenue for another six months—on March 20[th,] 2025. That's not just the first day of spring; it was Carol's birthday. She was a woman who brought spring into our lives and loved her precious few summers at Crooked Lake. During the longer winter nights and short winter days, we'll have plenty to do. And we will have enough blueberries for many celebratory brunches and evergreen memories to see us through until the days become longer than the nights.

By the time of the Spring Equinox, Harry will have harvested and bottled the golden rays of maple syrup, and George will be planning for and gathering ingredients for his Blueberry Maple Syrup Pilsner. The bushes at the special secret blueberry patch will still be covered in snow, but somewhere hidden from human eyes their life spirits will be nearing the end of their long winter sleep.

And I, looking down Eastern Avenue at the rising sun, will then begin looking forward to the day only two months away, when I'll park beside the Little Cabin in the Big Woods, welcomed by my co-tenants/fellow snowbirds, the robin and the hummingbird, and by the tiny pussy toes, gay wings, and forget-me-nots, the first flowers of ever-returning spring.

Acknowledgements

This collection of essays would not have been possible without the welcome assistance of many people. Thank you to Victor Volkman of Modern History Press, who encouraged me to undertake this project and guided me with patience and wisdom along the way. To editor Bob Rich goes my gratitude for his fine work. He not only spotted my many typos but offered valuable suggestions on how to clarify my writing. Deb Le Blanc, whose wonderful photos graced *Summers at the Lake* and grace this collection, has, for well over four decades, helped me and my family discover the many hidden wonders of the UP. To my UP friends, thank you for your support and encouragement over the years. My Crooked Lake neighbors added greatly to my enjoyment of my extended "Wild Blueberry Summers." And, finally, to Clare and Alberto and, in memoriam, to Carol – the Little Cabin in the Big Woods would not have been so wonderful a place without you.

About the Author

Jon C. Stott, Professor Emeritus of English at the University of Alberta, has spent most of his summers beside lakes – as a boy at Shawnigan Lake on Vancouver Island, Canada, and, since 1971 (when he was a professor at Western Michigan University), at lakes in Michigan's Upper Peninsula. Since his retirement, he has written non-academic books about minor league professional sports and the craft beer boom, along with retellings of traditional legends and folktales. Three of his "post-retirement" books have been set in the Upper Peninsula: *Paul Bunyan in Michigan: Yooper Logging, Lore & Legends* (The

Photograph by Claire K. Stott

History Press): *Summers at the Lake: Upper Michigan Moments and Memories* (Modern History Press); and *Yooper Ale Trails: Craft Breweries and Brewpubs of Michigan's Upper Peninsula* (Modern History Press).

About the Photographer

Deb Le Blanc, a retired plant ecologist, worked forty years for the United States Forest Service on the Hiawatha National Forest. Since early childhood, she has spent every summer at the family cabin beside the Indian River in the central Upper Peninsula. During her childhood years, she gained a passion for the out-of-doors and photography. Her photographs grace *Summers at the Lake* and *Wild Blueberry Summer*. She has restored the family cabin into a year-round home where she lives with her

family of furry kids, who often join her exploring the vast beauty of the Upper Peninsula.

Paddling a canoe into sunrise on the longest day of the year... watching a child take her first kayak ride with her father... gazing at a bald eagle, riding air currents high above the lake... chuckling as a hummingbird defends his feeder against intruders... dodging campfire smoke while burning marshmallows and telling scary stories to wide-eyed kids. These are some of the moments and memories depicted in *Summers at the Lake*. The essays—often humorous; sometimes tinged with a sweet melancholy--celebrate the people and events marking the progress of the

seasons—from the budding of the first green leaves of May to their falling, gold and scarlet, in September. These prose poems capture the joy of simple, lake-side living and quiet reflection.

"Jon Stott is a masterful storyteller. *In Summers at the Lake*, he shares memories that read like prose poetry. Each story takes us to a place of solitude and beauty and will stir pleasant memories of our own."

—Sharon Kennedy, author of
The Sideroad Kids: Tales from Chippewa County

"This gentle book by a gentle man is the kind that grows on you. Reading it will give you the same benefits as meditating in lovely surroundings in peace and calmness."
—Bob Rich, author of *From Depression to Contentment*

"*In Summers at the Lake*, much can be learned about life in the U.P. and its enjoyable places. You can explore the wonders of the U.P. while dipping your toes into the everyday experiences of life near Crooked Lake."
—Sharon Brunner, *U.P. Book Review*

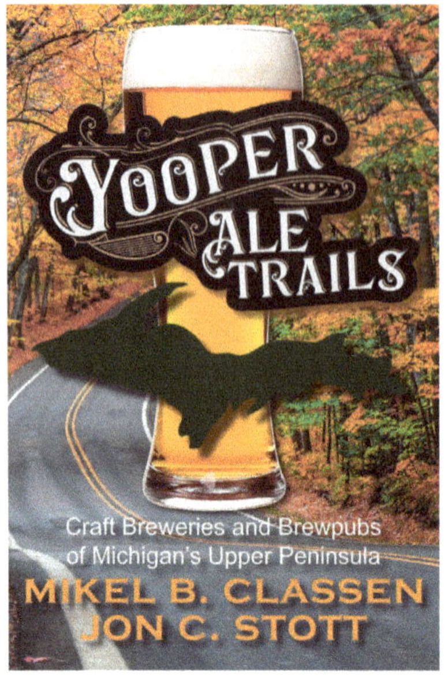

Follow *Yooper Ale Trails* to visit the 29 unique craft breweries and brewpubs of Michigan's Upper Peninsula. Choose from among eight different Ale Trails for your personal journey. Explore the backstories of the breweries, brewers and owners, along with tasting notes on each brewery's most popular beers. Jon C. Stott, award-winning author of five beer travel books, provides expert guidance for both craft beer aficionados and tourists to enjoy one of 170 locally-brewed lagers or ales after visiting the many scenic wonders of the U.P. Inside this book:

Tours are arranged geographically from the shores of Lake Huron, across the north of the peninsula close to Lake Superior and then east from the Wisconsin border to the shores of Lake Michigan.

Short essays on each brewery introduce you to the brewer's, the places their beers are served and the flavors of the beers themselves.

Complete contact details about each brewery and their available services (food, off-sales, accessibility, etc.), descriptions of beer styles with examples from UP breweries and a glossary of brewing terms.

Roadmaps for each ale trail and photographs of each establishment, making the breweries easy to find

"Cheers to the *Yooper Ale Trails*! Jon's book is a fun and easy way to get a close and detailed offering from each brewery. The beer tastings are the heart of the book, and you will readily see how much Jon enjoyed each and every visit. After reading this book, you will want to make your own journey!"

—Lark Carlyle Ludlow, Owner and Brewster,
Tahquamenon Falls Brewery & Pub

From Modern History Press